LEADERSHIP IN NEPAL

LEADERSHIP IN NEPAL

(A PILOT STUDY)

Nepal Centre for Contemporary Studies (NCCS)
In Cooperation of the
Embassy of Finland, Kathmandu, Nepal

by
Lok Raj Baral
Krishna Hachhethu
Hari Sharma

ADROIT PUBLISHERS
DELHI-110 053

Published by
ADROIT PUBLISHERS
C-8/2, Yamuna Vihar, Delhi-110 053
e-mail: akhilbooks@yahoo.com
Phone: 3266030

ISBN : 81-87392-23-1

Layout by
Sudhir Kumar Vatsa

Laser Typeset by
Nidhi Laser Point, Shahdara, Delhi.
e-mail: nidhi_vatsa@hotmail.com
Phone : 2825424

Printed in India by
B.K. Offset, Shahdara Delhi-110 032

PREFACE

Leadership like institutions and values is a crucial variable in politics and governance. Leadership qualities and roles are universal in nature and dimensions as all leaders should be endowed with certain new traits that set him apart from the common man. A leader is he who can continuously garrner confidence of his followers or the general public, take quick and bold decisions on the strength of his own understanding and objectivity, relate himself to the changing environment and context and, if possible, becomes visionary for the welfare of his people, country and the world at large. Such a broad definition may not necessarily be applied to the local conditions but for any leader to be different from others, he had to demonstrate his ability by maximizing popularity. All these credentials of a leader are however related to achievement criteria and are not found in the hereditary *khandani* or *kul gharana* concepts of leaders. Under the latter categories, leaders are born with ascribed statuses like the hereditary monarchical system where the eldest son of a king automatically succeeds his father irrespective of aptitude and qualities. His actual qualities would be put to test only after being declared a leader.

In our context and even in many other contexts where democracy has taken roots, those family tradition and lineage have worked greatly for thrusting leadership role on others. The son of a leader by passes all other prescribed ladders for becoming a leader in an organization turning other aspirants into by standers or silent members whose duty is only to show their habitual obedience to the new leader imposed from above. Added to such feudal values are the caste and class divisions that determine leadership role sin parties, parliament and in grass roots organizations. Nevertheless, the caste and family factors are being increasingly questioned by a wide spectrum of ethnic groups and intelligentsia. Political consciousness and educational level have started showing trends of assertiveness on the part of activists and citizenry trying to make the leadership roles to be responsive and sensitive to the public. Democratic openness and changes brought about by the present day society seem to be infusing a new culture into the making of leaders. The family and *khandani* underpinnings have to be approved either through the periodic elections or by adopting the system of "selectorate" to which other members of the group or party should accept. So even imposing a leader by the party on the grounds of family or on other criteria of ascription, popular acceptance is a must whatever incredible such artifacts might be.

Nepal needs to go a long way in preparing leaders on the basis of achievements alone as many other traits of traditional society continue to dominate the structures at all levels. Yet it is gratifying that about 60 percent members of parliament and sizable numbers of local leaders in elected committees are relatively new, despite question arising on continuity of many of them. Winning elections alone therefore cannot produce leaders despite elections being as one of the channels of throwing up leaders. It depends of politics either on their own merits or on their newly acquired legitimacy and resources.

The growth of leadership is a continuing process in a democracy. Since democracy provides opportunities and challenges to participants among whom leaders emerge, Nepal's progress is not disappointing if one takes into account the emerging pattern of leadership at the national and local levels. Coming as we did from a different political background and with high expectations of our central leaders, our perceptions and realities become incompatible when leaders fail to come up to such popular expectations, let alone the mitigation of genuine grievances. Moreover, democratic competition that prepares leaders would also not be adequate for its sustenance as both procedures and performances are integral aspects of democracy's survival. In Nepal, political leaders seem to stress much on formal structures rather than on striking a good balance between the structural parts and the functional (performance) aspects. Leaders are now under strain because of their neglect to people, because leaders in a country like Nepal need to be more sensitive to people's limited aspirations if not only to appear that they are always close to the people. When leaders become casual in their presence and are increasingly motivated by their selfish ends, popular perceptions also change.

Some key variables at the district and village levels were identified, administering both open-ended questionnaire and structured questionnaire methods for different categories of respondents. In addition to these methods, we have analyzed the composition, orientation and backgrounds of national and local leaders in order to show the differences between the past and the emerging trends of leadership in the country.

The present study would not have been possible without the assistance of the Embassy of Finland in New Delhi and Kathmandu. Ambassador of Finland to India and Nepal, Benjamin Bassin and Charge'd Affairs, Esa Hurtig, deserve our appreciation for encouraging us to take up such an important yet sensitive project. We hope Finland would continue to work with us in project concerning the consolidation of democracy in Nepal. The members of the field work team—Bishnu P. Adhikari, Ramesh Shrestha and Suman Aryal have done a commendable job by conducting surveys in the selected areas of three districts—Ilam, Dhanusha and Dadeldhura and tabulating data gathered from the field. Their expertise in survey research would also be of much use in the future. We want to encourage our young social scientists to be cognizant of recent developments taking place in social studies. Iswar Kharel of the NCCS has also helped in various ways in making this study a success.

CONTENTS

I

INTRODUCTION

Leadership is a one-way or mutual process of influence that obtains compliance. Leadership is sometimes treated as though it is virtually conterminous with management, but studies of leadership tend to emphasise various aspects of change, while those of management stress the status quo.[1] Historian, political scientist, psychologist and management theorists and scholars have produced extraordinary amount of literature over the years on the subject of leaders and leadership. There are countless biographies of leaders and empirical studies of leadership, but few have defined the conditions that produce leader or the qualities and skills that effective leaders must possess. Modern scholarly studies of leadership began around 1900 and focused on traits that distinguish great historical leaders from the masses. Related research, after the Second World War, began to emphasise the behaviour of leaders than the traits that distinguish leaders. More recently contingency theorists have proposed that the attributes and behaviour of effective leaders depend on situation—what challenges the leaders' face.

Trait Theory

Monarchies throughout the world practise generational succession. Kings or Queens simply transfer the leadership mantle to the first born child (primogeniture), whatever his

1. G. Yukl, *Leadership in Organization,* 3rd edn, Princeton, NJ : Englewood Cliffs, 1994.

or her qualifications, implying that leadership is genetically inherited. This royal model also figures prominently in the succession planing of many contemporary corporate business houses. The person who has accumulated the greatest experience and seniority is invariably the next in line. According to this theory, traits produce the leader. There are many theorists who, through various trait based studies, suggest the leadership qualities e.g. persistence, passion, conviction, integrity, authenticity, courage, vision, integrity, trust, curiosity, and daring. However, various researches have failed to uncover any statistically significant correlation between leaders' effectiveness and their personal characteristics.[2] Some suggest that the followers simply attribute certain qualities to a leader, based on their perceptions. Charismatic leadership is another variant of this model.

Behaviour Theory

Many management theorists define style—how the leader interacts with the followers- as the primary determinant of leadership effectiveness, and have given us a variety of classification schemes for leadership styles. Some writers characterise leadership as either political, directive, or value driven.[3] Others see commanding, manipulating, and paternalising as less desirable options than leadership style based on values.[4] Still others suggest that every leader or Chief Executive Office (CEO) have a characteristic approach to leading—strategy (focusing on future); human assets (managing one person at a time), expertise (valuing knowledge), and maintaining status quo or quest for a change.

Contingency Theory

While the behavioural models have been considered simple, the correlation between performance and style has

---

2. Ralph M. Stodgill, *Leadership,* Oxford : Oxford University Press, London, 1997, p. 14
3. *Harvard Business School, 1989.*
4. James O'Toole, *Leading Change,* London : Jossey-Bass, 1995.

been weak. Researchers in the leadership field while reviewing the earlier theories and models came to newer model known as the contingency model. This model suggests that leadership effectiveness is the result of three major variables: the nature of the task or what has to be done, the relationship between leaders and followers, and the power inherent in the leaders position. While contingency explanations are controversial, however, there are substantial empirical evidences to support them.

Other Theories and Understanding of Nepali Leadership

The wider acceptance of contingency theory began to wane in the 1990s with the adoption of political scientist James MacGregor Burns' important distinction between transforming leaders and transactional leaders.[5] Transactions represent the much of leader/follower relations. The transactional leader asks "What do you want?" and "What price are you prepared to pay for it?" The transforming leaders, on the other hand, satisfy the higher needs of the followers. They interact with followers to raise the organisation to a higher moral plane. Another similar model distinguishes between ordinary leaders, innovative leaders, and visionary leaders.[6] In the field of Political Science, the study of political leadership is still dominated largely by the Weber's typology. It is a very commonly held view that the Weberian categories of charismatic and bureaucratic-legalistic leadership are to be found in many political organisations, besides the traditional leadership emerging more from social structure than from the organisation itself. In this present study, our understanding of leadership is also conditioned by the Weber's model. In addition, as B.P. Koirala, the acknowledged charismatic but perennially controversial leader of Nepali politics, once said

---

5. James MacGregor Burns, *Leadership,* New York : Harper & Row, 1978.
6. Howard Gardner, *Leading Mind,* New York : Basic Books, 1995. In his most recent discussion of extraordinary individuals, Gardner differentiates between Masters (Mozart), Makers (Freud), Instrospectors (Virginia Wolf) and Influencers (Gandhi)

while defending his party's decision to accept the Constitution awarded by the King in his own terms in 1959, that "a leader is he who stands on the surface of realities."

A leader should have the combination of idealism and pragmatism because if he only adheres to dogmatic approach without taking into account the emerging trends and the ground realities, he would be misplaced and marginalized. Nevertheless, no genuine democratic leaders, whose ideological position has had impeccable record, would ever try to compromise his values in the name of pragmatism. Compromises to be made by a leader should not undermine the underlined spirit of democracy. It is a normative approach to politics but it cannot be exchanged with disguised opportunism or masked pragmatism that the Nepalis have had been observing in recent years. A charismatic leader has certain in-built characteristics and does not necessarily come by virtue of being in certain positions of power and authority, for "a charismatic leader may or may not hold a position of authority in a formal organisation". B.P. Koirala was a charismatic leader in his own right because even being deprived of power and formal positions, he continued to be a perennially dominant figure in Nepali politics. So was Ganesh Man Singh because of his courage and long struggle that he had undergone during his long political life since the 1930s.

Although charismatic leaders are prone to revolutionary spirit, their charisma also gets bogged down when constrained by hostile environment dominated by traditional or conservative aspects in interactive relations. In the opinion of Max Weber, charisma ' represents the main source of social and political innovation. "Yet, charismatic leadership tends to be authoritarian, if it is not suitably institutionalised showing 'direct loyalties with personal and arbitrary delegation of authority. Rules, norms and institutional behaviour are normally bypassed by the charismatic leader." A total overlap of the leader's image and party identity is the sine qua non of charismatic power."[7]

7. See Angelo Pancebianco, *Political Parties: Organisation & Power* London : Cambridge University Press, 1988 (English trans). pp. 143-45.

Is leadership an ascribed phenomenon? Or is it a rare quality inherited from birth as Plato stated, by way of explaining the characteristics of power elites (philosopher kings) that two aspects are crucial for being endowed with leadership virtues: temperament and training. If a person who is temperamentally ill-disposed to a leadership role, leadership thrust upon him hardly matter. A good training and socialisation process can also create leaders. Moreover, leaders are supposed to be imbibed with multi-dimensional facets among which initiative, confidence, boldness, vision, and organising capacity are paramount. Very few leaders are endowed with all of them as many manage to hold the mantle of leadership role with only some of these qualities. A good orator can also become a cheer leader but he may lack the statesmanship quality as demonstrated by a few leaders of the world as, Nelson Mandela of South Africa, has recently demonstrated such a rare combination of both of a cheer leader and of a visionary statesman who renounced his highest position after a presidential term of the country. Ganesh Man Singh of Nepal declined to accept the offer of heading the Interim Government in 1990 but later found himself indulging in the affairs of the state from outside the government which subsequently proved disastrous for the NC when the two leaders (Singh and G.P. Koirala, then Prime Minister) picked up the quarrel on spoils of government and on ego problems souring their personal and political relations. The leadership dereliction within the NC had telling effects on the party as well as on the stability of the government. Thus, the " problem of personality and predisposition", to cite Robert Dahl, though in a different context, seems to overshadow the democratic governance, devolution of leadership structures within parties and political environment.[8] Defining a political leadership, many try to relate leaders to power as it is "manifestly and essentially phenomenon of power". Leadership can also be

8. See Robert. A. Dahli, "Hierarchy, Democracy, and Bargaining In Politics and Economics" in Heinz Eulau, Samuel J. Eldersveld, Morris Janowitz., eds. *Political Behaviour*, New York : The Macmillan, 1956, (Indian edn. 1972), p. 88.

examined from a broader perspective when we see non-political leaders as being equally influential and encompassing in various non-political domains. Nevertheless, in political context, they command much deference and acceptability even without power. If one has a leadership capability, he can immediately switch his roles into political ones.

So from the impact points of view also, leadership role can be broadly explained in two types: transactional and transformatory. As Burns says, "one group of leaders, the transforming group, having a vision of the society, sets about doing something to implement that vision; the transactional leaders, on the contrary, merely operates trade-offs or exchanges one advantage for another".[9] Another types are 'real' leaders and 'office holders'.

In the Nepali context, today, most political parties' leaders are transactional in view of their overindulgence in short-term gains. Presenting themselves as mere power-seekers, most political parties' leaders in the post-movement period are generally perceived by the people as having been driven by a strong desire for power. Both intra-party and inter-party transactions were more or less confined to such games that could seldom be used for the larger interest of the people. Transactional leaders are not necessarily described as only self-seeking as leaders are put into central roles for carrying out the regular affairs of the state. Transaction therefore implies regular conduct of business between and among states and other agencies.

Transformatory leaders, on the other hand, bring about a qualitative change through the instrumentality of movement and actions. As it has been said: "Leaders who have come to power through a revolution, or military leaders who have espoused radical goals, have thus claimed that they would genuinely transform the conditions under which economic and social policy-making would take place in the country, seemingly beyond the demands of all but a small segment of their followers."[10]

---

9. As mentioned in Jean Blondel, *Political Leadership : Towards a General Analysis* London : Sage, 1987, p. 20.
10. *Ibid.*, p. 75.

From this perspective, can we term the 1990 movement as transformatory in nature and the leaders involved as revolutionary or "transformatory"? Could the movement leaders sanctify themselves from having been contaminated from self-aggrandisement? If one examines the nature, structure and dynamics of the political leadership patterns in the post-1990 movement period, it can be called a substantive change with which power elites could be circulated periodically on the basis of the Constitution based on the objective of the movement. Three general elections have already been held and all political parties had a chance to be in power. Yet, how far the underlined spirit of the movement has had been adhered to by the leaders and parties are subject to discussion. The manner with which the political leaders of various parties seem to be haunted by their complex and lack of confidence in carrying out radical socio-economic policies for transforming the status quo, they cannot be called transformatory leaders. Although compared to the past regime, politics is broad-based and integrationist, but political leaders involved in it have failed to live up to its ideals.

The other typology of leadership in Nepal is related to charisma as a phenomenon. Charisma is taken here in broad sense as the leaders having been graduated into leadership roles due to family background (*Khandan* or *Kul Gharan*) or through some ascribed social positions like former *zamindars* and local *Thalus*. Such links are often employed as a pass-partout for any role. So charisma as extra-ordinary qualities of an individual is not taken here, though in some individual leaders such qualities might be present.

Although the *Kul Gharan* and *Khandani* linkages can be well established in the local and central leadership patterns in Nepal, democratic exercises carried out since the 1950s to the end of '90s have significantly made inroads into the highly stratified leadership structures of various parties. The educational and political consciousness backed by the extended suffrage to the grassroots level has given a sense of empowerment to the general people during the local and national elections. The elitist bias continues to dominate the leadership composition at both the lower and central levels. Education, increasing influence of various ethnic groups and pressures being built from the lower level for greater participation of the deprived sections of society seem to be changing the structure. So, if we accept the elite structure as preordained by the societal and historical factors and which exist even today, then the existing leaders located in the Nepali politics come mainly from the elite groups. In the opinion of Bottomore, "the term elite(s) is now applied to the functional, mainly occupational groups which have a high status (for whatever reason) in a society".[11] Today's national and local elites who come from the traditional privileged sections of the society as well as from the new generation of educated people of caste and ethnic backgrounds are the sites for recruitment of leaders. Thus, the elite landscape is changing with the advent of participatory processes introduced during the thirty-years Panchayat regime that encouraged participation at all layers of the polity and in class and professional organisations from which many of today's parties' leaders have come.

Why study Political Leadership?

A systematic theory of the political process requires empirical data on the characteristics of various types of political decision-makers as well as investigation of their function within a variety of power contexts. Further, it involves the analysis of the formal and informal structures of those groups which, in order to meet the demands of their constituents, seek access to political power. Similarly, multiple political means and techniques condition the linkages between public, representative groups and political leadership namely, political party organisations and political communication. In a political democracy, the effective working of the system depends upon 'the interlocking functions of the agents and of the techniques of political power. This interlocking function must be recognised and

11. T.B. Bottomore, *Elites and Society,* London : Penguin 1964, p. 18.

studied scientifically to understand the working of the system.

The study of political leadership is as old as the study of politics. In addition, it has employed a variety of approaches borrowing from related social sciences. Since the early period of human civilisation, scholars have asked, debated, and sought to establish who governs or should govern, what are or ought to be the bases of political authority in a community or a society, and why and how some individuals obtain and exercise exceptional influence over the making of public rules and policies when others do not. Moreover, knowingly or unknowingly, these questions reflect comparative generalisations. What we remark here is an effective leader, an able statesman, a just administrator or, on the other hand, call a leader, a dictator, an opportunist, or a democrat, or a fraud, we make comparisons between what we see in a leader and what we expect of one.

As we are aware that earlier professional observers and practitioners of political leadership, from the time of Chanakya, Plato and Aristotle to our own, we have made it their special business to formulate such comparative generalisations. In most of the leadership studies, we find mainly two patterns—some of them are heavily descriptive, as in the case of biographies and historical works, while others are prescriptive studies which seek to establish principles of "proper" political leadership based on generalised assumptions about the nature of persons, society and authority.

"Politics by leadership"[12] is a major feature of modern political theory. Therefore, search for clear, precise and generally applicable analytical terms has been a major concern of contemporary efforts to study political leadership in various societies including Nepal. As social scientists have learned to inquire beneath the manifest aspects of leadership and discovering the relevance of numerous and complex factors, they have found it more difficult to agree on what leadership is and does. It is quite easy to distinguish between voters and

12. Lester G. Seligman, "The Study of Political Leadership" in Heinz Eulau et. al. *Political Behavior,* NY : The Free Press, 1956.

candidates in electoral studies, or recognise hierarchies in formal political organisation than to establish clear and operational boundaries that separate between leaders and followers in all situations. In the earlier case, the difference is clearly one of kind, in the latter, it is more likely to be one of degree. Followers may lead and leader follow and individuals who may be leaders in one situation may be followers in another.

Generally, political leadership is variously defined in contemporary social science literature as influence, authority, power and control over others. But how such concepts are to be defined and applied for comparative purposes remain a matter of considerable disagreement. Apparently identical or similar concepts—such as elite, authoritarianism and leadership role—may be defined in terms of very different operational criteria. On the other hand, various authors may provide very different conceptualisations of power, influence, authority, and control—in a quite similar operational term.

Some scholars identify political leadership with formal positions, offices, tasks, and functions along more or less traditional lines. Others emphasise performance: what leaders do and how they do it. Leadership is seen as the ability to guide and structure the collective behaviour pattern of a given group in a desired direction so that the decisions of the leader are implemented by group action. The leader is followed because he is loved, admired, respected, or feared, because he can coerce, persuade, or manipulate group members, because he can offer psychological as well as material rewards and punishments, or because compliance with his/her wishes is sanctioned by habit, traditional and legal-rational behavioural norms. Still other definitions are couched primarily in psychological rather than sociological terms. Here leadership is conceived as an attitudinal phenomenon in the mind of an actor who ascribes it to others, to oneself, or to both and responds accordingly to stimuli from his social environment. In short, varying definitions of leadership prevail and give rise to corresponding difference over what is the subject of study and comparison. In table one we have tried to summarise selected concepts and organizational criteria for the study of political leadership.

TABLE 1

Selected Concepts and Organizational Criteria For the Study of Political Leadership as applied to Present study of Nepali Leadership (Compiled from Leadership Literature)

Concept	*Definition*	*Operational Criteria*	*Example Area*
Leadership Authority	A relationship of inequality sanctioned by the legitimacy of leaders to make and enforce policy.	The nature and extent of legitimating group norms.	Elite and/ or mass consensus on rights and duties of formal positions, on means and ends of leadership behaviour.
Leadership control	The actual or perceived ability to provide or withhold benefits and apply sanctions.	Extent of leaders' ability to extract conforming group behaviour.	Comparing means of control (for example, coercion, manipulation) with compliance on the part of group members.
Leadership roles	The position of leaders. The behavioural 'style' of leaders His/her own perception towards the leadership position	Position in formal organisation and rights and duties associated with that position. Nature of interaction with other relevant actors. Expectation and sense of direction from the leadership position	Elected representative in various posts and positions. Behavioural ability to use coercion, manipulation, persuasion, etc. Whether leaders' functions are in conformity with group norms in the view of followers

Concept	*Definition*	*Operational Criteria*	*Example Area*
Personality of a leader	Individual, as distinguished from collective characteristics which influence attitudinal and behavioural pattern	Determination of personality, personal character—their sour, degree of adaptability and general impact on leader /follower	Learned expression of leadership, cultural standing and recognition, open etc.
Leadership recruitment	The process of leadership selection.	The variables which promote or hinder the acquisition of leadership. The general process through which leaders are chosen and displaced.	Social background, ambition, skills, charisma, respect, material values, connections. Electoral process, career patterns, revolutions, etc.
Performance of Leadership	Effectiveness and ability to perform duties and deliver goods and services promised	Representation in resource allocation process.	Promoting community development Securing governmental assistance Furthering political communication. Recruiting party members Mobilising electoral support.

The purpose of leadership analysis is intimately related to matters of conceptualisation and scope and thus constitutes another problem area. What should be the ultimate object of such studies is disputed among the scholars. Many insist that as social scientists, they are above all committed to seek knowledge and in their search for more precise and universally valid propositions have become increasingly wary of "value-laden" definitions and generalisations. What may be "common sense" in one society may be considered "nonsense" in another. In this present study of Nepali leadership, we are inclined to take a correspondingly relativist view of "democratic" and "non-democratic" form of leadership. Framing of research question and the nature of the problem one chooses to investigate may be dictated by a researcher's personal values, his search for the objective explanations, making predictions more free by subjective assumptions and normative value judgement if his or her data are to be collected and analysed "scientifically". For example, if one wants to study what constitutes a 'great leader' the person will have to consider the substance of definition in terms of the problem under investigation. To some, he/she may be a person who gets things done, such as furthering economic development or winning elections or wars; to others he/she may be a leader who maintains the "stability" of political system in the time of stress or who introduces major innovations into political processes.

However, this relativist approach has been strongly criticised by many, especially on two grounds. In the first place, the premise on which it rests is considered to be false. Social scientists cannot exclude their personal preferences from their investigations of political leadership.

In the second place, it is argued that students of political leadership have an obligation to employ their findings for public policy ends. Even assuming that they can and should strive for a maximum degree of objectivity in research and analysis, their ultimate purpose must be to study "important" political and theoretical moral problems. For instance, leadership studies ought to suggest ways to prevent crisis in the political system, promote democracy and development, and suggest what sort of person and leadership structures can most effectively advance the welfare of a particular society, community or political organisation. If they fail to do this, the claim for "scientific objectivity" allegedly represents but an evasion of the scholar's responsibility towards ones fellow beings.

The forgoing analysis of theories and approaches suggests that recent studies of leadership can be grouped in the following categories.

1. Leadership as social status-position.
2. Leadership as organisational functions and Institutional Positions.
3. Leadership as a personality type.
4. Political biographies and case studies.

Our aim of the present leadership study is to use all these categories into one since this is going to be a pilot study on political leadership in the post democracy movement-1990 Nepal.

Leadership here is exclusively confined to the peoples' elected representatives and the parties' office bearers. It attempts to explore a number of questions related to political leadership i.e., *(i)* concept, *(ii)* profile, *(iii)* sources of power and legitimacy *(iv)* strength and weakness, and *(v)* responsibilities and performance. Several hypotheses on each of the given component of the leadership can be advanced.

Hypothesis

Hypothesis 1. Leadership is a different quality, which is not ordinarily found in general people. Motivation, drive, skill and organisational ability are some of the qualifications.

Hypothesis 2. Leadership is not only related to personal quality. It emerges through an organisational process. Leadership building is, therefore, a complex process and a number of variable i.e., socio-economic background, personality, continuity, political socialisation, political attitude, social and political environments and internal organisational dynamics are prominent for making a leader.

Hypothesis 3. Most of the political leaders all over the world are drawn disproportionately from the people of higher socio-economic background.

Hypothesis 4. Political leadership is largely constituted by those people who have been traditionally enjoying power, by virtue of their higher position in social setting because of their economic power with big land holding and other financial assets, families and kinship ties, and through the cultivation of their connections with bureaucracy and other state power holders.

Hypothesis 5. Ethnic, untouchable and other minority groups of Nepal are either less politicised or the political parties have successfully integrated them into the democratic process.

Hypothesis 6. High caste groups, Brahmin and Chhetri have traditionally dominated the composition of political leadership of Nepal.

Hypothesis 7. Educated middle class largely constitutes political leadership in Nepal.

Hypothesis 8. Since political leaders of Nepal are products of parties' long struggle for democracy, a person's record of suffering, struggle and sacrifice in the past has contributed to his/her emergence as a leader.

Hypothesis 9. Legitimacy of party leaders especially at the central level is primarily determined because of their participation in the democratic struggle. However, leadership is sustained through popular acceptance.

Hypothesis 10. Career of a leader is determined by the factors of continuity, mobility and aspirations, which in turn help a person to be recruited into the leadership role.

Hypothesis 11. Kinship, lobby, factional ties, popularity among the workers and personal connection with senior leaders count much for putting a person into the leadership role.

Hypothesis 12. The main strength of many political leaders of Nepal is past contribution to the democratic struggle, whereas for the local leadership their constant interaction with the community at the local level is important.

Hypothesis 13. The popular support to the political party and leaders is largely determined by performance legitimacy of leaders.

Hypothesis 14. Crisis of Nepali leadership has emerged because of non-performance and of overall erosion in ethical and moral standards expected of a public personality.

In order to explore positions and characteristics of Nepali political leaders and to test the above mentioned hypotheses, a wide range of research tools and techniques i.e. archival research, experiences, observations, and field survey etc. have been applied in this study.

Methodology

This is an empirical study on political leadership of Nepal which lays the equal emphasis on both deskwork and field survey to collect information and data. Some scholarly works on theory of leadership, experiments of South Asian countries and historical perspectives of Nepali elite have been referred to back up our exploratory study and innovate thinking about the nature and characters of Nepali political leaders, who are working under the system of parliamentary democracy. This is, however, a pilot study undertaken in only 3 out of total 75 districts in addition to the selection of capital to cover up the central leaders. Only 21 leaders from the central level, 100 from the local level and 50 commoners were selected as respondents for questionnaire administration and selected personal interview. But for a broader perspective and leadership background, Nepal's historical, sociological and economic contexts have been adequately interconnected by way of making it a well-knit thematic study.

Sample Area

The areas selected for this study can be categorised into three tiers: *(a)* central level-Kathmandu *(b)* district level and *(c)* village/city level. Ilam, Dhanusha and Dadeldhura districts were selected through purposive sampling but taking into consideration of broad representatives of different ecological zones, caste/ethnic groups and influence of political parties are taken into account. If Ilam is a politically sensitive district of eastern hill, Dhanusha is a central Tarai district with distinct socio-cultural background and Dadeldhura is a Far-western hilly district. Among the three major ethnic groups of Nepal, the Rai-Limbu community from Mongol race dominates Ilam; the *Madhesi* (plain group) constitutes as majority community in Dhanusha; and the Brahmin and Chhetri castes , from the Aryan race are predominant in Dadeldhura, in terms of settlement pattern of various caste/ethnic groups in the given districts. The local elections of 1997, in which the undivided Communist Party of Nepal (Unified Marxist-Leninist) or in short CPN-UML swept in many areas, are taken as measurement for the justification of above sampled districts in terms of political influence of different political parties. Accordingly, the CPN-UML dominates local politics of Ilam; its splintered group, the ML constitutes majority among the elected members of Dhanusha's District Development Committee (DDC); and the Nepali Congress (NC) retained its stronghold in Dadeldhura district.

Each of the three-sampled districts was divided into rural and urban areas to cover up grass roots leaders working at village and city level. Accordingly, all wards of the municipality, from each sampled district, were considered as one "urban cluster." The rural cluster consists of four adjoining Village Development Committees (VDC) of each sampled district.

Sample Size

Three major political parties— the NC and the CPN—UML and the Rashtriya Prajatantra Party (RPP) representing different ideological backgrounds and identity are considered in selection of respondents of this study. The respondents can be divided into two groups: *(a)* political leaders of three parties holding posts either in the parties' formal organisations or in elected bodies or in both and, *(b)* citizen of sampled districts and villages/ cities. The first type of respondents consist of 21 central level leaders (parliamentarians, ministers and members of party's Central Committee), 50 district level leaders (elected representatives of DDC and members of the party's District Committee) and 50 grass roots level leaders (people's representatives of VDC/Municipality). The total number of second type of respondents is 50.

Research Techniques

Two major research tools—questionnaire administration and personal interview—were applied during the fieldwork. A set of structured questionnaire was used to get an interview with 100 village/city and the district level local leaders. The number of parties' representation among the 100 respondents, selected for questionnaire administration, are CPN-UML 44, NC 33, RPP 17 and others six. The unequal distribution of respondents in terms of parties' representation is not a deliberate choice but reflections of parties' strength in local politics across the country in general and sampled districts in particular are noted. Out of total 100 respondents selected for questionnaire administration, 21 respondents were reselected for personal open-ended interview. Besides this, 21 central level leaders—seven from each of the NC, CPN-UML and the RPP—were chosen for in-depth interview. Thus, 42 leaders of whom 21 from the local level and 21 from the central level leaders were chosen for in-depth, open-ended interviews. A separate set of structured questionnaire was administered to 50 citizens to cross-check peoples' perspective on the overall status of leadership situation, specially the nature, character and functions of political leaders of Nepal.

The picture of research methodology—sample area, sample size and research tools—applied for field study is presented in the table below.

TABLE 2

Sample Area, Sample Size and Research Tools

Sample Area	*Interview*				
	NC	*UML*	*RPP*	*Others*	*Total*
Central Level	7	7	7	—	21
Local Level					
Ilam	2	4	1	—	7
Dhanusha	4	2	1	—	7
Dadeldhura	3	2	—	2	7
Total	16	15	9	2	42

Sample Area	*Questionnaire Administration*					
	NC	*UML*	*RPP*	*Others*	*Total*	*Citizen*
Ilam	7	22	5	—	34	17
Dhanusha	14	12	8	—	34	17
Dadeldhura	12	10	4	6	32	16
Total	33	44	17	6	100	50

II

LEADERSHIP IN COMPARATIVE PERSPECTIVE

What kinds of persons are considered for leadership in a political party? One widely acknowledged and empirically tested fact is that most party leaders all over the world are drawn disproportionately from the people of higher socio-economic backgrounds.[1] But, only few from such privileged groups have chance to place themselves in the narrow space of leadership ranks. For, several other factors influence the leadership building process. Leadership is an outstanding quality i.e. superiority in intelligence, character, skill and power, and standard setters to the social values.[2] Superior knowledge and outstanding personality are not enough since the party leadership building is an organizational process. Two

1. Enormous studies on political parties resulted in a common finding that leaders are usually from a higher socio-economic background. Examining the correlationship between a political position and social status, Robert D. Putnam postulated agglutination theory of elite composition and specified education, wealth and social status as "political resources" behind the formation of leadership. Sees Robert D. Putnam, *The Comparative Study of Political Elites,* New Jersy : Prentice-Hall Inc., 1976.
2. The Classical elite theorists like Pareto, Mosca, Harold Lasswell etc. strongly emphasize on personal quality of individuals in leadership, position. See for Pareto and Mosca's approaches to leadership in Peter Bacharach, *The Theory of Democratic Elitism : A Critique,* London : University of London Press Limited, 1969; Harold Lasswell, *Who gets What, When and How,* New York 1936.

contrasting views are found in organizational process of leadership building. One is the constitution of oligarchy by a small group of leaders who carefully recruit some new leaders through cooption.[3] The other view is that the career development in the party, from being a sympathizer to achieving the status of a leader, is determined by the factors of continuity, mobility and aspiration.[4] In fact, leadership building is a complex process and a number of variables i.e. social background, personality, continuity, political socialization, social and political environments, internal organizational dynamics etc., interplay in selection of persons to the position of the party leadership.[5] The relative importance of any one or few among several variables could be different from one country to another that depend upon social setting, political history and party's internal dynamics of a particular country.

In South Asian countries where the origin of political parties was closely associated with independence or democracy movement, a person's record of political struggle is still more important than any other factors in building the party leadership. The core central leadership in most of political parties of India and Sri Lanka has been constituted by freedom

3. See for oligarchic theory of leadership formulation, Robert Michael *Political Parties : A Sociological Study of the Oligarchical Tendencies of Modern Democracy,* New York : The Free Press, 1968; Maurice Duverger, *Political Parties,* New York : John Wiley and Sons, 1954; Angelo Panebianco, *Political Parties : Organization and Power,* Cambridge : Cambridge University Press, 1988.
4. Samuel J. Eldersveld is the pioneer scholar who contradicted the oligarchic theory of leadership formation and propounded the theory of the circulation of elite in political parties. Se Samuel J. Eldersveld, *Political Parties: A Behavioural Analysis,* Chicago : Rand NeNally, 1964.
5. For more integrated and comprehensive approach of leadership building, see William E. Right, ed, *A Comparative Study of Party Organization,* Ohio : Carles E. Merrill PUblishing Company, 1971; Lewis Bowman and G.R. Boynton, "Activities and Role Definitions of Grassroots Party Officials", *Journal Of Politics,* February 1966, pp. 121-43, Lewis J. Edinger, *Political Leadership in Industrialised Societies : Studies in Comparative Analysis,* New York : John Wiley and Sons, 1967; Kay Lawson, *Comparative Study of Political Parties,* New York : St. Martin Press, 1976.

fighters or descendants of heroes of independence movement. But, concern shown to the recruitment of party local leadership in post-independence time has demonstrated that the socio-economic background of aspirants has been considered as the most crucial factor for election purpose. Most political parties, Indian National Congress in particular, were adapted to the local power structure through building local leadership from among those who had local power and influence. The local authority system is still largely based on caste, ethnicity, land, wealth etc. The people from high caste groups and big land holding have therefore continued to hold their domination in composition of the party local leadership[6] despite the introduction of universal adult suffrage has theoretically opened up opportunities to all, including unprivileged groups to rise in power structure. Rather, it is through excessive politicization of caste, community, ethnicity and religion with which the people from low caste, untouchable and tribal groups, and minority communities not hitherto represented or least represented are successfully asserting political power.[7] But Pakistan and Bangladesh are least affected from emerging trends of unprivileged movement. The party local leadership in these countries is largely constituted by those people who have traditionally enjoyed power and influence by the virtue of their higher position in social setting, their economic power with big land holding and other financial assets, their family and kinship ties, and through cultivation of their connection with local administrative officials.[8] The more domination of

6. See Myron Weiner, *Party Building in a New Nation : The Indian National Congress,* Chicago : University of Chicago Press, 1967; Stanley A. Kochanek, *The Congress Party of India : The Dynamics of One-Party Democracy,* Princeton : Princeton University Press, 1968; B.S. Bhargava, *Grassroot Leadership : A Study of Leadership in Panchayat Raj Institutions,* New Delhi. Ashish Publishing House, 1979; V.M. Sirikar, *The Ruling Elite in a Developing Society,* New Delhi : Orient Longman Ltd., 1970.
7. See Atul Kohli, *Democracy and Discontent : India's Growing Crisis of Governability,* Cambridge : Cambridge University Press, 1991.
8. Dalem Ch. Barman, *Emerging Leadership Pattern in Rural Bangladesh* (Unpublished Ph.D. Thesis), Jaipur : University of

traditional forces in local authority structure of Bangladesh and Pakistan relates to the fact that the feudal elements are more powerful in social and economic structures of these two countries with military being the powerful component of such structures. The feudals, army and bureaucracy remain more influential in the total power structures and their impacts in the party leadership are obvious. Nevertheless, the numerical strength is in favour of young and middle aged educated people from middle class backgrounds in the total composition of leadership in party organizations and in the parliaments of Bangladesh and Pakistan.[9] Pakistan's case is more striking in view of the highly stratified political structure.

Socio-Economic Background and Elite Structure

In Nepal, the high caste group—Brahman, Chhetri—and the upper caste Newar—have dominated the leadership of most political parties, including the NC and the CPN-UML, the two largest parties of the country. It shows the pre-eminence of high caste groups in social, economic, administrative and political structures of the country. The table below shows the ascendancy of the hill caste groups over other ethnic communities in composition of political elite in Nepal in the past.

The root of hill caste domination in Nepali politics lies with social stratification in the Hindu Kingdom of Nepal into four groups—Brahmin, Chhetri, Vaishya and Sudra as prescribed by the Hindu Vedic ethos based on division of labour. In order, Brahmin and Chhetri are placed at the top with their ritual positions: Chhetri as a ruling class and Brahmin

---

Rajasthan, 1983. A.K.M. Golam Hoosain, *Bangladesh Nationalist Party : A Political Analysis* (Unpublished Ph.D. Thesis), Rajasthan : University of Rajasthan, 1984; Abbas Rashid & Shahid Karder, "Baseline Assessment of Political Parties and Party System in Pakistan", an unpublished article presented to National Democratic Institute for Internal Affairs, Washington, August 1997.

9. Rounaq Jahan, *Bangladesh Politics : Problems and Issues,* Dhaka University Press Ltd., 1980; A.K.M. Golam Hoosain, *Ibid;* Abbas Rashid & Ahahid Kardar, *Ibid.*

TABLE 3

Ethnic/Caste Representation in the Legislatures

	Democracy		*Panchayat*	
Ethnic/Legislature	1959	1964-79	1981	1986
Hill Castes	62.4	72.0	57.78	66.44
Brahmin	27.5	23.5	14.81	21.16
Chhetri	31.2	35.5	34.82	38.68
Newar	3.7	13.0	8.15	6.60
Hill Tribes	15.6	14.9	21.48	17.51
Plain Group	22.0	11.4	18.10	13.86
Untouchable	—	1.0	2.6	2.19
Total	100	100	100	100

Source: Harka Gurung, "Representing An Ethnic Mosaic," *Himal,* Vol. 5, No. 3, May/June 1992 and DREFDEN, *Report on the Study and Research on the Local Elections in Nepal, 1992,* Kathmandu: DREFDEN, 1992.

as priest and advisor of ruler. Such a religion-based hierarchical social structure was legally reinforced and practised as the state protected ideology with the enactment of Civil Code in 1854 further classifying several caste and ethnic groups into three broader categories in ascendancy order: *(a) Tagadhari* (sacred-thread wearing castes—Brahmin and Chhetri) at the top, *(b) Matwalis* (alcohol drinking castes and ethnic groups) in the middle, and *(c) Sudra—achhut* (impure and untouchable castes) at the lowest position.[10]

The social setting of Nepal has thus been monopolized by the Brahmin and the Chhetri castes, yet being a member of the high caste group alone is not adequate for political fortunes. From the mid-18th to early 19th century when Nepal emerged as martial state with its unification and territorial expansion,

10. For understanding of stratified hierarchical social setting of Nepal in diverse perspectives, see P.R. Sharma, "Nepali Culture and Society : Reflections on Some Historical Currents" in Kamal P. Malla, ed., *Nepal : Perspectives on Continuity and Change,* Kathmandu : CNAS/TU, 1989, pp. 139-68; Dor Bahadur Bista, *Fatalism and Development : Nepal's Struggle for Modernization,* Calcutta : Orient Longman, 1991.

the personalities who were in forefront got opportunities in constituting political elite. In addition to *Chhathar* families (Pande, Pant, Arjyal, Rana, Bohara and Khanal), which rendered outstanding service to the unification of Nepal and accompanied Prithivi Narayan Shah while shifting capital from Gorkha to Kathmandu, some other Chhetries from Thapa, Basnyat, Kunwar and Thakuri families, who commanded the task of territorial expansion in the post-unification period, dominated the composition of royal courts of Shah rulers.[11]

With the advent of Rana rule in 1846, other factors also came into play for elite composition, though the martial tradition became an exclusive domain of the family oligarchy. As all top ranking posts in administration, military and politics were monopolized by the Rana family members, the ascriptive criteria—birth, blood, lineage, family and kinship ties predominated the elite formation. Under the highly centralized Rana regime, the Newar, original inhabitants of Kathmandu valley, joined the Brahmin and Chhetri as members of elite groups with their presence in the outer circles of the Rana power structure. The elite formation from the central to the local level during the Rana period as practised in the pre-Rana period was a two-way process. The commoner received status by demonstrating their loyalty, obedience, submission through *Chakari* (obsequitous attendance) to the rulers. The rulers in turn distributed *Jagir* (job), conducted *Pajani* (annual reshuffling of service personnel) and granted *Bakshis* (gift and reward), solely on their own discretion setting a new tradition of institutionalizing favouritism and nepotism in administration.

Turning Nepal from oligarchic state into a democratic one following the end of the Rana regime in 1951, the exclusivity of ascriptive criteria of birth and family in elite formation were broken, though not fully replaced by the new one. During a decade of multi-party democracy—1951-1960, both the NC and the Communist Party of Nepal (CPN) appeared as

---

11. See Mahesh C. Regmi, *Kings and Political Leaders of Gurkhali Empire 1768-1814,* Hyderabad : Orient Longman, 1995.

pluralistic organizations in composition of their rank and file from different social and economic backgrounds.[12] Nevertheless, the educated middle and upper class people from high caste groups—Brahmin, Chhetri and Newar—predominated in the party central leadership, the unprivileged section of the society i,e, *Madhise* (plain people) and hill tribal groups not hitherto represented in power structure of the country entered into political elite circle with their sizable numbers. The representative of *Madhise* and hill ethnic group was 15.5 and 26.3 percent in the government and 22.0 and 15.6 percent in the parliament respectively in 1959.[13] Even though most ministers, parliamentarians and party leaders, irrespective of their castes or tribes or Tarai groups, were constituted by the people of middle and upper ranks in social status or economic position or combination of both in their respective communities, they acquired the positions through achievement criteria i.e. attainment of education, involvement in the 1950-51 anti-Rana revolution, association with and service to political parties etc. The representation in the party leadership from feudal elements as well as peasants decreased substantially in the post-1960 period under the partyless panchayat system. Hence the leadership of NC and communist parties were largely constituted by the educated middle class.[14] Yet, the pluralistic character of party leadership, with high caste domination, in terms of social composition,

12. See Anirudha Gupta, *Politics in Nepal : A Study of Post-Rana Political Developments and Party Politics*, Bombay : Allied Publishers, 1964; *Nepalese Interviews*, Delhi : Kalinga Publications, 1997; Bhuwan Lal Joshi and Leo E. Rose, *Democratic Innovations in Nepal : A Case Study of Political Acculturation*, Berkeley : University of California Press, 1966.
13. Quoted in DREFDEN, *Report on the Study and Reserach on the Local Elections In Nepai 1992*, Kathmandu : DREFDEN, 1992, p. 7.
14. See for leadership pattern in Nepali Communist parties, Bhim Rawal, *Nepalma Samajbadi Andolan : yashko Udbhab, Vikas ra Bartaman Abastha*, Nepal : Samana Prakashan, 1984 (2044 V.S); Leo E. Rose, "Communism Under High Atmospheric Conditions : The Party in Nepal" in Robert A Scalapino, ed., *The Communist Revolution in Asia*, New Jersey : Prentice-Hall, 1965, pp. 346-53.

remained unchanged and the contribution of such elite groups to oppositional politics against authoritarian panchayat system had become an important factor for party recruitment.

Some simplistic examples could be immediately advanced in the case of the failure of the partyless regime led by the King. In the preceding royal regime too, crucial issues and agendas dealing with economy, polity, education palpably failed as a result of the loosening grip of the centralised power structure, despite such national issues being emphasised by no other persons than the King. When King Mahendra noticed that his radical economic programmes had flopped despite his much touted land reform programme and the policy of economic diversification extending Nepal's foreign trade to third countries beyond India, he had declared the 1970s as the decade of development. Similarly, the New Education Policy introduced under the initiative of King Birendra (then Crown Price) floundered after a while. In the later period of his rule, despite the King's personal involvement in developmental affairs, economic growth in terms of income generation and human resource development did not increase. And politics did not obstruct them in view of the nature of the polity. Such a dichotomous situation that eluded the desired objective of development in all its ramifications—economic development during the partyless regime, and institution building and socio-economic growth under the new democratic regime—point to some basic flaws of governance.

Concentration of power in the personalised leadership of the King and the culture of *chakari* and sycophancy that made the palace secretariat more powerful than the government headed by the Prime Minister bred a variety of corruptions and systemic aberrations turning some of the system functionaries' rebellion thereby giving rise to the anti-regime forces to mobilise as well as mount a mass movement. External environment, changing fast in favour of democracy, boosted the sagging morale of dissidents whose efforts got tacit support of the disenchanted *panchas* (*former* regime supporters).

After the restoration of democracy in 1990, the pattern of leadership formation has changed. The achievement criteria of service to the party has largely been considered in recruitment of the party leaders instead of dominance of the ascriptive criteria of birth and family lineage. This, however, does not ensure nor is it essential that the distribution of political elites would be in proportion to social stratification. But the leadership composition in democracy is expected to be fairly representative in character giving enough space to diverse social groups. Different social groups have also become more assertive for their roles in democracy than in the previous authoritarian regime. And a competitive party should consider the pluralistic social structure of the country while building and expanding its own support bases. The more the party's ranks and files pull together diverse social elements, the more broad would be the party social base.

It was not a new phenomenon if one looks at the ultimate fate of any authoritarian rule in the world because of its failure to take a definite course of its development. Nor could such a regime develop its own intrinsic capability to cope with challenges fuelled by its all pervading failures. But why democracy in a country like Nepal seems to be facing similar failures despite the popular legitimacy it has received through the periodic elections held under the Constitution prepared on the ground of political consensus among the major political forces including the King? It has been felt by a wide intellectual circles and political audience that most problems and even crises encountered by the country are due to dismal failures of leadership roles in the post-1990 period of democratic restoration. The ten-years exercises in multiparty democracy [1990-2000] have shown that democracy as a principle and democratisation as a process of building democratic institutions with the procedures as well as dynamism are different subjects, though principles constitute the operational agendas for democratisation. In Nepal, parties and leaders knew democracy as a principle for whose achievement they engaged in struggles whatever the consequences.

Failure of democratic governance could be ascribed to the social and economic backgrounds of politicians in general ranging from die-hard monarchists to the so-called democrats and progressives despite the involvement of parties, leaders and their followers in movements launched in the name of democracy and development. While the former regime supporters could maximise favours of the regime through various channels and actions and had been able to amass wealth and reach pinnacles of offices, if not power, the latter (party elite) did emulate the same behaviours to which they had denounced to the hilt in the past. The social and economic bases of all elites of Nepal are similar and their political socialisation in authoritarian and feudalistic norms and values remain unchanged. Inasmuch as they appeared to be elitist in the typical Nepali background and orientation, their proneness to the same political cultural traditions and norms is evident under the present dispensation. "This pattern was in consonance with ancient Hindu scriptural requirements that the rulers of a state should always be recruited from the Kshatriya, or warrior, caste and that they should exercise their political functions with the advice and consent of the Brahmans, the intellectual elite and spiritual preceptors."[15]

It is interesting to observe that in the period just on the eve of the fall of the Rana regime in 1950 and later during the democratic period, the political leadership roles have had been provided by the Brahmins. In today's political parties, the domination of Brahmins and Chhetris continues to the chagrin of various low caste groups and ethnic communities of the country. All the major political parties have Brahmins as the apex leaders who invariably share power with the Chhetris (Kshatriya), with one lone exception of a Newar Prime Minister (Vaishya) during the last phase of the partyless regime. As it has been pointed out:

> Today, one can find Bahuns in every part of the political and ideological spectrum. Within their ranks, there are conservatives, liberals, monarchists, republicans, socialists, Marxists, Maoists, extremists, and anarchists. Neither is there indication towards the conservative

15. Joshi and Rose, *op.cit. 12,* p. 23.

> end of this ideological spectrum. They are represented in substantial proportions in all segments. This is quite a radical transformation.[16]

And against such historical and existing socio-economic and political backgrounds, we have to grapple with the problems of leadership in Nepal. Our conceptual formulation has been based on the universally accepted criteria as well as on variables that broadly represent the existing reality of the subject. How local leaders also reflect the broad historical composition and dynamics of elitist politics thus weaving a running thematic unit of analysis has been presented with the help of field studies conducted in three sample districts of the country.

The main focus of the present study is to establish a correlationship or no-relationship between the governance and leadership either in the government or in opposition because of the failure of democratic leadership in impressing the general populace about their capacity as governing elites. Most of the leaders who had struggled for democracy and human freedoms and also languished in prisons or remained perennially defiant for achieving the set objectives—democratic governance with equity—as also enshrined in the Constitution framed by them have demonstrated that they not only lack commitment to the processes of democratisation but also become deviant from their objectives. Although, many exercises which they had not perhaps envisaged during their struggle have come to the fore with all sorts of aberrations and pitfalls, the democratic system on the whole has proved that there can be no better alternative to it if the elite involved in such exercises show minimum courtesy to its operational norms. As much as the general people's expectation has been dashed by their undemocratic behaviour and aggrandisement, people still have a faith in the integrationist democratic system. Yet, sometimes it becomes difficult for us to differentiate the elites and democratic processes, as both are exclusive to one another. Our objective is only to concentrate on the actors but not on the ingenuity of democratic order.

---

16. Prayag Raj Sharma, "Bahuns in the Nepali State", *Himal*, 7 : 2 : 1994.

Environment of Nepali Leaders

Nepali political elites operate in a kind of contradictory environment because of the long and entrenched tradition of authoritarian political culture punctuated by the impinging social and economic values inherited by the Nepali society. On the one hand, Nepalis want that their governments should be swift and progressive in dispensing justice and social equity reminiscent of the old monarchical and personalised trends of leadership roles, on the other hand, they want all the ingredients of modern democracy with its impeccable functioning. Nepalis were also accustomed to quick changes of governments every now and then during the post-Rana period and later during the thirty-years' monarchical rule. Persons designated by the Rana rulers or later on by the Monarch could also use their delegated power. It was a direct rule as power was concentrated in the hands of rulers who in turn could delegate such powers. Some analysts of such a nature of politics and of the methods and styles of running the governments have preferred to compare it with the patrimonial system as posited by Max Weber. According to such schematic discharge of functions, personality factor, and informal relations with the power elites and accountability to none other than the ruler are the principal characteristics. "Informal contacts take precedence over formal procedures and power vests in the hands of persons or personalities rather than in institutions."[17]

Today, the spirit of patrimonial system prevails despite the democratic Constitution and the sub-laws created within it. The leaders and their followers who also constitute the political elite have seemingly inherited these trends demonstrating that they operate within the twilight zone of democratic governance and authoritarian culture as handed down to us from history and tradition. A peculiar similarity between the political behaviour of the post-Rana party elites

---

17. See in detail, Rishikesh Shaha, *Essays in the Practice of government of Nepal,* Delhi : Manohar, 1982, p. 115.

and others who found the new democratic system incompatible to their traditional interests such as the monopoly in land tenure and the *birta* systems and that of the post-1990 political elites was evident while undergoing the constitutional exercises. Its reasons were not far to seek.

First, the political orientations of most of Nepal's leaders were diametrically opposite with the NC championing the cause of the multiparty system *a la* the British model where monarchy and full fledged democracy could co-exist, while the Communist Parties of Nepal had its Marxist-Leninist elan with intermittent modifications for coping with the neo-Maoist trend of China. Ideological heterogeneity and adjustment of principles according to the time and situation seemed to be the operating norms of the post-Rana politics. Conflict-prone and divisive in nature, the Communist movement turned out to be fragmentary with each individual leader articulating juxtaposed ideological lines during the long haul of royal rule since the coup in 1960. Among the radical variants was the *Jhapali* group whose closest parallel was the Naxalite movement across the Indo-Nepal border around a small town—Naxalbari in North Bengal, India. The Jhapali group covered a long distance by the time it joined the movement for the restoration of democracy initiated by the NC in 1990.

Similarly, the Pushpa Lal and Mohan Bikram groups who had all along been advancing the republican form of government were significantly transformed after the death of the former in late 1970s though the latter continues to be radical in order to show its distinct political identity amidst the groups. However, this group wants to be different from the ongoing Maoist violent activities reminiscent of the old Jhapali movement that had adopted the "campaign of liquidation of class enemies" through the violent Maoist methods as they used to call. Other personality groups that numbered more than a dozen also wavered inasmuch as they adopted whatever strategies and tactics they found either for spreading disaffection for the regime or in search of adjustment with the regime.

The non-Left groups had more or less moved closer to

the NC presenting it as the sole representative of the democratic movement. But the NC turned out to be a political maverick during its long struggle for democratic system with its hard-core leaders taking occasional plunges into regime politics and the reasons advanced by them for such moves were untenable. The NC leaders were seemingly lacking political consistency in their ideological and strategic orientation. Outmanoeuvred and outwitted by King Mahendra and later by King Birendra, the NC leaders compromised too much in the late 1950s through the 1960s and '70s and '80s with taking contradictory stands that could seldom serve its objective. In 1959, its core leaders departed from its principal objective of a constituent assembly as per the Delhi-Compromise then reached between the Rana rulers, the King and the NC with the Indian government's mediation. In 1959, King Mahendra after consolidating his power, offered to award a Constitution on his own terms, not on the basis of the Royal proclamation made by King Tribhuvan. Vested with all discretionary powers, the King became sovereign and all-powerful that eventually proved to be detrimental to the multiparty system in 1960.

The NC is basically a status quo party in practice, if not in nuances, because, reading into its past history and also into the behavioural patterns of its leaders, the NC leadership seems to be reluctant in providing a progressive mould in their activities except in 1959-60 when the party under the leadership of B.P.Koirala adopted some progressive land reform measures. Ideologically, the leadership went too far in accepting the then partyless Constitution for its "further development" whereupon the King granted amnesty to its hard-core leaders then living in self-imposed exile in India and later released B.P.Koirala and Ganesh Man Singh after ascertaining their acceptance of the party's offer of "loyal co-operation" to the King.[18] Subsequently, B.P. Koirala's armed revolution that eventually turned into "reconciliation with the

18. How the Nepali Congress leaders went on changing their stands occasionally has been adequately dealt with by Lok Raj Baral in *Oppositional Politics In Nepal,* New Delhi : Abhinav, 1977, Chap. 4.

King" in 1976 were all constraints of environment or of strategic compulsions that prompted the leaders to be contentious as well as contradictory. Sometimes, Koirala even went to the extent of rejecting the Gandhian non-violent methods for a country like Nepal where only the armed movement was possible as was done in the 1950 anti-Rana movement but at other times, he offered co-operation to the King with the same spirit and confidence while simultaneously advocating for violence in the early 1970s. In 1990, the NC under the command of Ganesh Man Singh successfully launched the anti-regime mass movement, with the co-operation of other parties.

The foregoing narration explains the ideological ambiguity and strategic swings of leaders who defy uniform pattern of behaviour and culture. Leaders took decisions on their own without undergoing broad-based prior consultation or they could prevail easily on their followers for complying with their decisions. Inasmuch as focus on personality rather than on organisation was the core of analysis, dealing with such a complex and intriguing aspect of leadership role in relation to Nepal's environment and the constraints impinging on it cannot be discussed in isolation. Are the core leaders the product of environment or leaders themselves can create a conducive environment for maximising their underlined objectives—realisation of basic freedoms and needs of general people in order to empower them as sovereign in the real sense of the term and spirit as underlined by the Constitution of the Kingdom of Nepal.

Can an ideology of any leader and the lingering gaps in operational norms based on any "ideology" prompt us to infer any definite idea on the leadership role in Nepal? In broad sense, political parties and leaders committed to constitutional process based on universally accepted criteria of good governance such as accountability, transparency and efficacy for showing performance legitimacy is our preordained agenda. In this context, political leaders who abide by the principal underpinnings of the Constitution can be called ideologically guided though their functional ideologies might vary from party to party. Conceptualising the two broad types of ideologies, one which is integrationist in nature and is ordinarily inviolable, and the other is functional. The former category is intertwined with the constitutional process based on minimum consensus as is the Constitution of the Kingdom of Nepal, a product of the movement, and the latter are changeable according to leaders' priority and focus. If the NC wants to identify its major agendas of governance with its socialistic orientation—whatever insipid and amorphous it might be, it can accordingly formulate policies to which other parties may or may not subscribe. In the same vein, the CPN—UML, as its resolutions passed by the General Conference *(Maha Adhibeshan)* show that it can design its own operational agendas with the objective of being more radical and different from other parties but such operative part of its ideology is not expected to contravene the spirit of the Constitution of the country.

At the one end, ideologies are "normative, ethical, moral in tone and content", at the other end, " they have a body of sacred documents (constitutions, bills of rights, manifestos, declarations), and heroes (founding fathers, seers and sages originators and great interpreters)". It has been said "all ideologies, like all other beliefs, imply an empirical theory of cause and effect in the world, and a theory of the nature of man."[19] From the former perspective, the democratic exercises carried across ten years' period are seldom ethical, moral and normative because of their failures to strictly adhere to the tone and tempo set by the spirit of the mass movement. On the contrary, the so-called democratic leaders turned out to be principal deviants as and when the opportunistic alliances were forged with the sole objective of grabbing power and positions. The extent to which they fought for the spoils of power did not show an iota of principled politics so much so even the leaders who had all along been championing the cause of value-based politics turned into the major defaulters of the constitutional spirit. Although such ugly behaviours displayed against principles failed to get popular approval, many sinners

19. Robert E. Lane, *Political Ideology,* New York : The Free Press, 1962, p. 15.

also succeeded in getting into the parliament through the electoral devices skilfully manipulated by them during the elections.

So if the leaders take pride in violating rather than in protecting the minimum norm of public life, democracy degenerates into a ritualistic affair. Is this phenomenon percolated into other layers down to the grassroots level or is it only a trend at the central level needs to be examined. Our findings based on a number of variables seem to substantiate some of our hypotheses put forth in connection with studying local leaders' perceptions and understandings of the central leaders. Moreover, since the "centrality of Kathmandu" (capital) continues to be centre of all political activities concerning local, regional and central levels, producing a new breed of elites migrated into the capital, leaders representing their constituencies in different districts have a tendency of being transformed into yet another category of capitalelites. Those representatives who come from a variety of social, economic and local backgrounds are disposed to belonging to the new set of Kathmandu elites. Such a conversion tendency had been observed by King Mahendra while announcing the Back-to-Village National Campaign (BVNC) in 1968 according to which the regime functionaries at all levels were to conform to ten-point guidelines including their adherence to the "partyless" spirit. Other points were concerned with development. But, as any other personalised programme, the BVNC also lost its credibility soon after its implementation. Programmes of decentralisation of power both under the royal regime as also during the post-1990 democratic polity also received only ritualistic treatment because of the strong tendency of centralisation of power through modern Nepali history. While implementing the various acts of decentralisation, "creeping trends of centralization" were/are always ubiquitous in the polity and administration regardless of the nature of the system.

So any study on Nepali leaders is difficult without relating it to the pervasive centralising tendencies. Such intermixing phenomenon fails to delineate the boundary between local and national affairs as all national level leaders confront the local problems during elections and on other occasions local leaders favour central intervention in order to get things done. And only the local leaders communicating with their superior leaders at the Centre constitute the core of local leadership throwing the others at the backyard of local politics because of the limited channels of communication for them. So the process is not as interactive as the essence of participatory democracy demands in a plural set up. For pluralism" emphasises the active side or politics and adaptive learning by means of public participation at multiple levels of politics and in diverse social and political bodies."[20]

In the centralised ambience, the pluralist participants too tend to resemble non-participants due to missing links between the electorate whose major preoccupation is about their own local issues and agendas to which their own leaders can seldom address unless they get the nod from above. How participatory democracy becomes futile if a political process lacks co-ordination and interaction has been adequately discussed by a host of political analysts. Although participation of the maximum number of people "increases democracy" but, in absence of commensurate institutionalisation that demands "co-ordination and control, too much participation may lead to "political decay".[21] The ten-years of pluralist exercises at both local and central levels lacked institutional development in content which significantly also hampered the emergence of leadership role based on systemness.

The location of leaders in actual practice can be found in the capital thus defying all norms of decentralisation of power. Nepalese are also temperamentally ill-disposed to both institutionalised and decentralised behaviours of leaders demonstrating that after having been elected to different posts, they emulate the same practices as bequeathed by the authoritarian leaders. Thus, in a sense, all are authoritarian in

20. David Apter, *International To Political Analysis,* Cambridge : Massachusetts, Winthrop, 1970 (Indian edn.), p. 293.
21. See Samuel P. Huntington, *Political Order in Changing Societies,* New Haven, Conn. : Yale University Press, 1968, p. 79.

nature and practise smacking of the Rana and Shah rules under which the peripheral elites too could exercise power and authority delegated to them from the higher layers.

Politics of Co-option

Political parties in Nepal have invariably given grounds to the personality traits that enable the central leader or top leaders function as the apex of an organisation. If a leader, who acts on his own volition and unfettered authority bestowed on him by yet another superior leader, nominates some subordinates to fill up the posts—vice-president, secretary, joint secretary and members of central committee—he seems to apply his own subjective criteria because of the absence of inner-party democracy. Some are also hereditary successors and some others are the favourites of the apex leaders. Political parties have devised, not evolved, a "variety of automatic, quasi-automatic, and discretionary techniques" for nominating the "eligible aspirants" for leadership roles. Sometimes, it goes with seniority considerations, at times the juniors become the *kakhe* (*lap*-leaders) who cannot take any initiative without the indication of their superiors.[22] It resembles the *Mansaya* system (to prepare memos according to the will of the superior) of the Nepalese bureaucracy. While explaining the composition and styles of functioning of the Nepalese bureaucracy during the partyless Panchayat period but which can also be applied to the present time because of the continuity of such trends, it has been said that actual decision-making took not within the bureaucracy but elsewhere. "It was characterised by formal loyalty to the hierarchy but informal loyalty to the feudal power brokers."[23]

The mechanisms of selection of leaders seem to exist in all

22. Daman Nath Dhungana has coined this word by way of explaining the behaviours of the so-called second and third generation leaders of the Nepali Congress. Based on the interview on November 13, 1999 at Nepalgunj.
23. See Govind R. Agrawal, "Decentralization for Rural Development in Nepal" (Monograph), Kathmandu : CEDA, Tribhuvan University 1986, pp. 11-12.

political parties but with certain variations and degree. Top party leaders are believed to have been favoured by the lower level electorates but the process ends up with what is called " selectorate composed of party's most senior leaders."[24] How the selectorate operates and what credentials prompt the selectorate to determine the cooption of leaders needs to be understood. In a highly centralised system dominated by personality and lineage and nepotism and favouritism, ascriptive criteria get better preference over achievement, though the top leaders can hardly ignore the leadership potentials of some lower rankers in the party. The ratio between ascription and achievement is 60-40 with the fulcrum tilting in favour of the latter. Among the other credentials of selection of leaders can be organising ability, intelligence, hard work and dedication to the party cause, family and factional ties, patron-client affiliations, and ethnic and regional considerations.[25]

Leadership Selection

A marked differences are there among the NC, the CPN-UML, and the RPP in their formal rule of leadership selection. The NC constitution prescribes a presidential system in its organizational units at all levels. According to the NC's amended constitution, its Village/Town Committee is constituted by *(i)* an elected president *(ii)* vice-president, secretary and treasurer appointed by the president from among the committee members *(iii)* several elected members, including one representative from each ward *(iv)* president's nominees and *(v)* the party' MP of concerned VDC (Village

24. The electorate system is not entirely a new phenomenon. In Western democratic countries, parties adopt both the methods of selection and election. Even while selecting the members of the British cabinet, ministers are selected by the parliamentary party despite it being the Prime Minister's own prerogative. In most Western democracies, selection system operates at various levels. "...selectorates for parliamentary seats are typically composed for local activists, whereas the selectorate for cabinet posts is restricted to national party leaders". See in detail, Putnam *Op.Cit. I*, pp. 52-55.
25. *Ibid.,* pp. 60-63.

Development Council) /Municipality as ex-officio member.

The NC's District Committee is constituted by *(i)* an elected president *(ii)* vice-president, secretary, joint-secretary and treasurer appointed by the president from among the District Committee members, *(iii)* some elected members—one from each parliamentary constituency, and *(iv)* president's nominees not exceeding fifteen.

The NC's Central Committee consists of *(i)* president elected by majority of not less than 50 percent from the total members of the National Convention, *(ii)* vice-president, general secretary, assistant general secretary, treasurer appointed by the president from among Central Committee members, *(iii)* five elected members—one from each five development regions—voted by the delegates of concerned region to the National Convention, and *(iv)* president nominees not exceeding 25.

The CPN-UML has adopted parliamentary model in formation of all tiers of its organizational structure, that participants of the party conference elect committee members first and then the elected committee members elect their leaders i.e. chairman, (general) secretary, deputy secretary and office secretary. According to the CPN-UML's constitution its Village/Town Committee members are directly elected by the party's organized members at the time of the party's Village/Town Conference. Some top posts—secretary and deputy secretary—of the Village/Town Committees are indirectly elected by VCMs (Village Committee Members) /TCMs (Town Committee members).

The CPN-UML's District Committee consists of *(i)* elected representatives, one from each area, *(ii)* elected members from general seat not exceeding six, *(iii)* nominated members (by the District Committee executives) not more than 25 percent of total elected members, and *(iv)* secretary, deputy secretary and office secretary voted by elected District Committee members.

The CPN-UML's Central Committee is constituted by *(i)* 35 elected members from the delegates of the National Congress, *(ii)* chairman and General Secretary voted by elected

Central Committee members, *(iii)* and nominated members not exceeding 25 percent of total elected members.

The RPP stands between the NC and the CPN-UML and adopts a mixed system of presidential and parliamentary forms in recruitment of its rank and file leaders. According to the RPP' constitution, its Village Committee is constituted by *(i)* one elected chairman, *(ii)* seven elected members, *(iii)* seven nominated by chairman, and *(iii)* vice-chairman Secretary, assistant secretary and treasurer appointed by chairman among the committee members. The same procedure is applied in constituting its Town Committee by total 13-15 members.

The RPP's District Committee is constituted by minimum 15 to 27 members in addition to ex-officio members. It consists of *(i)* one chairman elected by delegates of the party District Conference, *(ii)* 50 percent elected members, *(iii)* 50 percent nominates of chairman, *(iv)* Ex-officio members i.e. MP, chairmen of Constituency Committees, and *(iv)* vice president, secretary, assistant secretary and treasurer appointed by chairman from among the committee members.

The RPP's Central Committee has 41 members. It consists of *(i)* one chairman elected by participants of the party National Convention, *(ii)* 20 elected members, *(iii)* 20 nominees of chairman, and *(iv)* vice-chairman, general minister, assistant ministers, treasurer, and spokesman appointed by the party chairman.

In recent years, political parties seem to introduce both the election and selection systems for filling up the vacancies in different tiers of organisations. The Nepali Congress (NC) and the CPN (UML) and now CPN (ML), the RPP have made the provisions for village, district and General Assembly before recruiting leaders into the higher echelons of organisations.

Drawing the membership of the NC is rather loose and contrasts with that of the CPN-UML and the ML. The NC that worked as the only credible democratic party after the 1960 coup was a kind of movement that transcended most liberal organisations and public opinion. Many parties represented in the 1959-60 parliament had already joined the NC, while many people had over the years developed certain sympathy for its democratic struggle. In the post-1990 politics also, many former regime supporters and functionaries became Congressmen and women who were later described as *chaite* Congress (functionaries of former partyless regime who joined the NC after the triumphant movement), a derogatory word used by the so-called' genuine congressmen. Since many of such new entrants could influence the top leaders of the party, they, in fact, excelled the 'real' Congressmen in getting important leadership roles in the party. Their bargaining capacity was also taken into account while distributing seats to parliamentary elections or to some other crucial party posts. Conceivably, the NC's ideology and credential of a genuine democratic party are being questioned both by its opponents and by its own members. Yet, viewed from the perspective of its own flexibility and of Nepal's unique political reality which has had accepted a kind of reconciliation policy between the King, the active and supreme leader of the dismantled regime and the movement parties, such accommodation was an imperative for the parties committed to the constitutional process.

Nevertheless, too much compromise made by the senior leaders of the party did give rise to doubt to the democratic credibility of the NC. Many NC supporters, transcending party members, intellectuals and others, refer to the word *panchangress* in order to show a process of dilution between the NC and the former partyless regime. What is more noteworthy is that even the party president takes serious note of the vanishing spirit of the Congress and leaders and workers inasmuch as they hardly show any spark of democratic zeal towards the organisation, and government which has a comfortable mandate to govern for five years.[26]

26. Remarks made by the party president during his visit to Janakpur on November 18,1999 have adequately focussed on how the NC is afflicted by its inertia. Urging the Party men to be more aggressive and active for pointing out the failures of the government, G.P. Koirala admitted that the leaders and workers of the party were either frustrated by the leadership role or were motivated by their own interests. See *Kantipur*, November 19, 1999.

Constitutionally, the CPN-UML has the central party organs such as National General Assembly (NGA), Central Committee, Central Advisory Committee, Central Judicial Committee, Central Auditing Committee, and the National Assembly. It has been arranged that the Central Committee nominates members of those committees. The CPN-UML has introduced the bottom-up system whereupon senior leaders depend upon the votes of the congregated members of the NGA. Among the local party committee organs, zonal or special committee, district committee, district assembly, constituency co-ordinating committee, area committee, branch committee, primary committee, party cell, and general assembly are mentioned.

The structural pattern of the CPN (ML) that had split from the CPN-UML in early 1998 has given a new nomenclature—politburo—to the Central Committee. It has more or less the same types of functions as are mentioned in the CPN-UML's Central Committee. It seems that the NC has adopted a presidential structure, while the two communist parties prefer to be parliamentary inasmuch as most of their organs are elective bodies, despite their adherence to what Lenin had said "democratic centralism" and ' inner party democracy'.[27]

Organisationally, the other Left-parties who fought elections with a view to "exposing the exploitative capitalist parliamentary system" are not entirely different from one another despite their emphasis, whatever fallacious they might be, on their own respective rationales for participating in the pluralist system as underlined by the Constitution of the Kingdom of Nepal, 1990. After a fierce intra-party debate on whether to adopt the *Bahudaliya Janbad* (multiparty people's democracy) or *Naulo Janbad* (new people's democracy), as respectively advanced by the late Madan Bhandari and C.P. Mainali, the CPN-UML accepted the former to which the advocates of the latter school of thought subscribed until the party split in 1998. Yet, the CPN (ML) led by the *Naulo Janbadi* group continues to swear by the Constitution of the country

27. For details, see *The Constitutions of the CPN-UML and the CPN (ML.).*

contrary to its populist and contradictory statements on its ultimate objectives. Because of its failure to undercut the organisational structures of the CPN -UML after the split, the CPN (ML) not only fared badly in the 1999 parliamentary elections, but it also failed to win a single seat. Although many senior leaders of the erstwhile extreme Left movement had joined it, the people might have felt that they were the main culprits for splitting the CPN-UML.

From leadership point of view, however, both the CPN (UML) and ML are prone to schisms and conflict due to personality factors which had all along been the root cause of party splits since the early 1960s through the 1970s, '80s and '90s. Such schisms are a general phenomena of all the parliamentary parties, though the split of the NC has had been avoided time and again due to the flexibility of the two apex leaders—G.P. Koirala and K.P. Bhattarai.

The Rastriya Prajatantra Party's (RPP) birth was marked by split when the two strong personalities who had served the dismantled partyless regime as prime ministers and their respective supporters, all of whom were also senior ministers during the partyless era, could not reconcile their differences over the posts and leadership roles. In the beginning, the two RPPs had four seats in the first House of Representatives 1991-94, though they succeeded for merging the two RPPs into one by distributing the organisational posts somewhat proportionately. However, the former Prime Minister Surya Bahadur Thapa became the President, while a new post was created for another former Prime Minister Lokendra Bahadur Chand to upgrade his status in the merged party. But the inner-party conflict continued to strain their working relations during the phase of coalition politics when no major parties received requisite mandate to govern. As a consequence, the RPP, which emerged as a third party with 20 seats in the 205-member House of Representatives, its leaders claimed that the key to making and breaking governments lay with the RPP. Such assertions came true with both the then undivided CPN-UML and the NC who had respectively become first and second party in the lower house courting the RPP for power. Although the RPP got two opportunities to lead the coalition governments, the coalition politics that made the senior RPP leaders ambitious also led to the split of the party in 1997. Now the RPP led by Surya Bahadur Thapa emerged as the third party next to the NC and the CPN-UML in the 1999 general elections giving an absolute majority to the NC to govern.

Like the NC and the CPN-UML and the CPN (ML), the RPP, too, makes the *Kendriya Mahadhibeshan (Central* Convention) as the most important body that elects the president of the Party. The Central Convention is composed of representatives from the districts, electoral constituencies, Central Council *(Kendriya Parishad),* nominees of the Central Committee and other representatives of the party's ancillary organisations.[28] Besides such structures of the four major parties, there are other professional and occupational wings such as *Tarun Dal* (youth organisation) and the *Nepal Vidyarthi Sangh* (Nepal Student Union), Nepal Women Organisation, Trade Union Congress, Peasants organisation etc of the NC. Other professional organisations—Teacher, Lawyer, Medical Association, and Engineers' Association—are also close to the NC. Similarly, the Left parties recruit their leaders from various organisations. The RPP is rather weak in expanding its base to professional groups though the RPP has followed the pattern of other parties.

Structure of Leadership

The structure of leadership in the Nepali political context is related to social and economic backgrounds, and the sites for locating the elites who provide leadership roles are not far to seek. Basically, the sites for the recruitment are not uniform as the historical leaders who have had occupied central positions in the parties like the NC came from both movements either in India or in Nepal. The first generation of leaders were socialised in the Indian Nationalist Movement

28. Sridhar Khatri, "Political Parties and Parliamentary Process in Nepal" in POLSAN, *Political Parties and Parliamentary Process in Nepal : A Study of Transition Phase,* Kathmandu : POLSAN, 1992, p. 43.

and in the anti-Rana movement within the country. Today's apex leaders—G.P. Koirala and Krishna Prasad Bhattarai—are the products of anti-Rana movement of the 1950s—and continue to dominate the party. Ganesh Man Singh, the spirit and initiator of the 1990 anti- royal regime movement came from the background of pre-1950 political oppostion. The three identified leaders of the so-called second generation namely Sher Bahadur Deuba, Ram Chandra Paudel, and Sailaja Acharya are the products of the 30-year old movement launched against the partyless regime after 1960. Although none of the three has been designated as the elected President or vice-president or General secretary of the party but one—Shailaja Acharya, who was once nominated as vice-president by G.P. Koirala. But all of them have occupied high governmental and legislative offices by becoming Prime Minister (Sher Bahadur Deuba), Speaker of the House of Representatives (Lower House) (Ram Chandra Poudel) and the Depurty Prime Minister (Shailaja Acharya). However, they are more or less ascribed posts whose popularity test remained elusive because of the overriding decision of the two septuagenarian leaders. How would they fare without the support of the two leaders is yet to be seen. Given the reality and stronghold of old leaders, particularly G.P. Koirala, it seemed implausible to infer any conclusion on the popularity of junior leaders.

Nevertheless, the blessings of the old leaders are not likely to determine the leadership role within the NC, as a few instances in the past have demonstrated that some leaders had been able to win the central committee membership from five developmental constituencies and the fight for some seats was fierce. The victory of one member—Vijaya Gachhedar, a Tharu by ethnic identity, against Prakash Koirala, the eldest son of B.P. Koirala had shown that democratic competition was being practised vis-à-vis the climbing up of political ladder through family and personal routes. At the local levels, competitive politics takes ugly shape with party members indulging in groupism whose only objective is to besmirch the image of one's own party rivals. So in each district, local units are perennially conflict-torn during the local and general elections leading to the expulsion and suspension of various party functionaries.

Since the NC was a movement party for many years, the apex leaders distributed party posts. The presidential system of the party has inhibited the other junior rankers to contest unless the senior leaders backed them. Such an arrangement seemed to have been made for organisational homogeneity lest the fragmentation of the party in an ambience where party ideology is gradually being replaced by extreme form of individualism. Such an invading trend has not only given a jolt to the unchallenged leadership of the party but it has also counter-balanced the factional feuds by the shelter provided by the two senior leaders. In fact, it appeared as a political see-saw that withstood the offensive role of one another. And the junior leaders of the NC preferred to join either camp in order to save themselves. However, one of the positive aspects of the NC was that the party never took any precipitous decision towards split as the CPN-UML and the RPP did following the clash of senior leaders.

The composition of leaders of the three major parties—the NC, the CPN-UML, and the CPN (ML)—is based on traditional social hierarchy—caste, class and education. The high caste groups dominate all layers of party organisations, while the representation of ethnic and oppressed communities is marginal. In all representational patterns, such a disparity is evident though it is not deliberate in view of the long historical tradition that espoused caste and class stratification in all areas of government. Figures quantified on the basis of composition of party hierarchies and parliaments show that the same pattern continues despite the opportunities of participation given to various communities in those organs.

The ascendancy of the hill caste groups over other ethnic communities in Nepali politics[29] has remained unchanged,

---

29. For ethinic contents in understanding Nepali politics and elite, see Federick H Gaige, *Regionalism and National Unity in Nepal,* New Delhi : Vikas Publishing House, 1975; Prayag Raj Sharma, "Ethnicity and National Integration in Nepal : A Statement of the Problem", *Contributions to Nepalese Studies,* Vol. 14, July-December 1987, pp.

TABLE 4

Caste/Ethnic Composition of Parties' Central Committee Members *

	NC		*UML*		*RPP*		*Total*	
Variables	*No*	*%*	*No*	*%*	*No*	*%*	*No*	*%*
Hill Caste Group								
a) Brahmin	18	58.1	25	71.4	5	17.2	48	50.5
b) Chhetri	6	19.4	6	17.0	7	27.5	19	20.0
Newar	1	3.2	2	5.7	2	6.9	5	5.3
Others	—	—	—	—	—	—	—	—
Hill Ethnic Group	3	9.7	1	2.85	8	27.9	13	13.7
Terai Caste/ Tribe Group	3	9.6	1	2.85	6	20.7	10	10.5
Others	—	—	—	—	—	—	—	—
Total	31	100	35	100	29	100	95	100

* Members of parties' Central Committee is broken into caste/ethnic groups by authors themselves.

irrespective of fundamental changes in political systems of the country, as it has shown, in the table 4 above by the figure of ethnic distribution of the parties' Central Committee members and their representatives to the House of Representatives.

The aggregate data of the Central Committee members of the NC, the CPN-UML, and the RPP reveal that Brahmin alone

23-30, "How to Tend This Garden" *Himal,* May/June 1992, pp. 7-9, Harka Gurung, "Representing An Ethnic Mosaic", *Himal* (op.cit) pp. 19-21; Dilli Ram Dahal, "Ethnic Cauldron, Demography and Minority Politics : The Case of Nepal", Dhruba Kumar, ed., *State, Leadership and Politics in Nepal,* Kathmandu : CNAS/TU, 1995, pp. 148-170; Krishna B. Bhattachan, "Ethnopolitics and Ethno-development : An Emerging Paradim in Nepal", Dhruba Kumar, *Op.Cit.,* pp. 124-147; Ananta Raj Poudyal, *Nation Building in Nepal : A Case Study of the Post Revolution Period 1950-1981* (Unpublished Ph.D.Thesis), Kathmandu : Tribhuvan University, 1986; "Nepal : Ethnicity in Democracy" Lok Raj Baral, ed., *South Asia : Democracy and The Road Ahead,* Kathmandu : POLSAN, 1992; "Nation, Nationalism and Some Issues of National Consensus", *Contribution to Nepalese Studies,* Vol. 18, No. 1, January 1991.

constitutes more than half of total central leaders of these three parties. Chhetri comes as the second dominating caste with its share of 20 percent, followed by the Hill Ethnic Group (13.7 %), the Tarai community (10.5 %), and Newar (5.3 %) in total 95 central leaders of the given three parties.

It seems that the RPP, in sharp contrast to the two major parties—the NC and the CPN-UML- has taken care of sociological balance. Its 29-member Central Committee is composed of eight Chhetris, five Brahmins, eight persons from the hill ethnic groups, five from the Tarai, and one Newar. On the contrary, the Brahmins dominate the NC with 18 members, six Chhetris, three Hill Ethnic Group members (Gurung, Tamang and Rai), three from the Tarai and one Newar from the Kathmandu Valley. It is interesting to note that all the three female members and the two top-ranking office bearers —president and general secretary—belong to the Koirala family. The CPN-UML, like the NC, seems to have ignored the ethnic balance. In its ten-member Standing Committee (the apex body) all are Brahmins and one Chhetri. Among the Central Committee members elected by the Sixth National Convention, 23 are Brahmins, six Chhetris, one hill ethnic community member and one from the Tarai.

Similarly, a comparative view of representational pattern, given in the table (5.1 to 5.3), shows caste and ethnic composition

TABLE 5.1

Caste/Ethnic Composition of Members of House of Representatives, 1991

	NC		*UML*		*RPP*		*Others*		*Total*	
Variables	*No*	*%*	*No*	*%*	*No*	*%*	*No*	*%*	*No*	*%*
Hill Caste Group										
a) Brahmin	47	42.7	29	42.02	2	50.0	2	9.1	80	39.0
b)Chhetri	22	20.0	9	13.04	2	50.0	2	9.1	35	17.1
Newar	6	5.5	6	8.7	—	—	2	9.1	14	6.81
Others	1	0.90	—	—	—	—	—	—	1	0.5
Hill Ethnic Group	9	8.2	18	26.1	—	—	7	31.8	34	16.0
Terai Group	25	22.7	7	10.2	—	—	9	40.9	41	20.0
Total	110	100	69	100	4	100	22	100	205	100

TABLE 5. 2
Caste/Ethnic Composition of Members of House of Representatives, 1994

	NC		*UML*		*RPP*		*Others*		*Total*	
Variables	*No*	*%*	*No*	*%*	*No*	*%*	*No*	*%*	*No*	*%*
Hill Caste Group										
a) Brahmin	40	48.2	46	52.3	4	20.0	1	7.1	91	44.4
b) Chhetri	15	18.1	11	12.5	7	35.0	5	35.7	38	18.5
Newar	2	2.4	9	10.2	—	—	2	14.3	13	6.3
Others	1	1.2	—	—	—	—	—	—	1	0.5
Hill Ethnic Group	7	8.4	12	13.6	3	15.0	2	14.3	24	11.7
Terai Group	18	21.7	10	11.4	6	30.0	4	28.6	38	18.5
Total	83	100	88	100	20	100	14	100	205	100

TABLE 5.3
Caste/Ethnic Composition of Members of House of Representatives, 1999

	NC		*UML*		*RPP*		*Others*		*Total*	
Variables	*No*	*%*	*No*	*%*	*No*	*%*	*No*	*%*	*No*	*%*
Hill Caste Group										
a) Brahmin	52	47.3	39	54.2	—	—	4	33.4	95	46.3
b) Chhetri	19	17.3	8	11.1	5	45.5	3	25.0	35	17.1
Newar	6	5.5	4	5.6	2	18.2	1	8.3	13	6.3
Others	2	1.8	—	—	—	—	—	—	2	1.0
Hill Ethnic Group	11	10.0	13	18.0	1	9.1	—	—	25	12.2
Terai Group	20	18.2	8	11.1	3	27.3	4	33.3	35	17.1
Total	110	100	72	100	11	100	12	100	205	100

* Total members of House of Representatives is broken into caste/ethnic groups by authors themselves.

of members of the House of Representatives in the last three general elections held after the restoration of democracy in 1990.

The resentment at the Brahmin dominated politics is increasing. But interestingly, it has negative impact so far as the caste/ethnic composition of the members of the House of Representatives (HOR) in the last three tenure of parliament is concerned. The number of Brahmins in the HOR increased from 39 percent in the first parliament (1991-94), 44. 4 percent in the second (1994-1999), and 46.3 percent in the third. Chhetri has almost same strength: 17.1 percent, 18.5 percent and 17.1 percent in the HOR in the corresponding periods. The representative of Newar is also stable i.e, 6 percent in all three general elections. The representative of the Hill Ethnic Group decreased from 16 percent to 11.7 percent to 12.2 percent in 1991, 1994 and 1999 parliamentary elections respectively. A similar trend appear in the case of the Tarai community that its representatives declined from 20 percent to 18 percent to 17 percent under the time of review period.

Such an increase in Brahmin's representation and decrease of other communities—is substantiated by the statistics of individual parties. Brahmin constituted only 42. 7 percent among the NC's members of the HOR in 1991-1994 but increased to the figure of 48.2 percent in 1994-99. This figure slightly decreased into 47.3 percent in 1999 elections. The representatives of Chhetri among the NC members of the HOR went down from 20 percent to 18 percent and 17. 3 percent respectively in the same period. Newar representatives decreased by 2.4 percent within the NC in 1994, 5.5 percent in both 1991 and 1994. Hill Ethnic Group slightly improved their strength (among Congress MPs) from 8.2 percent to 8. 4 percent and 10 percent in 1991, 1994 and 1999 respectively. A reverse trend appeared in the Tarai community since the Congress MPs from the Tarai decreased from 22.7 percent to 21.7 percent to 18.2 percent respectively in the corresponding periods.

Brahmin's domination is more distinct in composition of the CPN-UML members of the HOR as it constitutes 42.02 percent in 1991 but increased to 52.3 percent in 1994 and 54.6 percent in 1999. Chhetri appeared as the loser i.e. from 13.04 percent to 12.5 percent and 11.11 percent in the first, second and third parliaments respectively.

The numbers of Newar representatives increased from 8.7 percent in 1991 to 10.2 percent in 1994 but decreased to 5.55 percent in 1999. The numerical strength of Hill Ethnic Group fell from 26.1 percent in 1991 to 13.6 percent in 1994, but slightly improved in 1999 with its representation of 18.5 percent. Increase of the Tarai community among the NC members of the HOR was marginal from—10.2 percent in 1991, 11.4 percent in 1994 and 11.11 percent in 1999.

The RPP showed a unique case about the caste/ethnic composition of its members of the HOR. In 1991, among its four MPs , 50 percent came from Brahmin and Chhetri backgrounds. But the strength of these two caste groups had plummeted to 20 percent and 35 percent respectively in 1994. The Hill Ethnic Group and the Tarai community had 19 and 30 percent respectively among the RPP members of the HOR in 1994. Surprisingly, not a single Brahmin of the RPP succeeded in getting into the lower house in 1999. The Thakuri/Chhetri domination in the RPP reflected the representation pattern having 45.5 percent Chhetris in its total strength in the HOR. The representation of Hill Ethnic Group and Tarai community decreased respectively to 9.1 percent and 27.3 percent in 1999.

The leadership role of women is negligible and it, in fact, contrasts with the spirit of the Constitution. At least five percent women should be enlisted as participants in all layers of elections but the political parties seem to make it more ritualistic by trying only to fulfil such a Constitutional provision but failing to encourage more women participation in all units—village, city/town and national parliament. The patriarchal structure and ethos of the Nepali society and the conflicting interpretations of the women participation handed down to the present seem to have put women at an inferior category. Though no legal constraints are in existence for greater women participation, lack of education, opportunities provided to women and mentality have worked as stumbling blocks for leadership of women. It could be seen that whatever women used to be co-opted and encouraged to contest elections through the official Women Organisation during the partyless regime is surprisingly decreasing during the ten-years' exercises of party politics. It did not mean that the former regime had ensured the maximum participation of women in offices, in legislature, in government etc., but they had the provisions for being active through such ladders as were prescribed by the Constitution.

But such representation in legislature from the Class Organisations were discontinued following the Third Amendment to the Constitution of Nepal in 1980 that changed the indirect system of representation to the national legislature into direct election based on adult franchise.

The predominance of male in politics, however, has continued throughout the modern Nepali history. A sociological study has thus shown the great disparity existing between the male and female representational pattern in the Nepali politics. It states: "Under the partyless Panchayat polity, for instance, in the 1981 elections, out of a total of 1096 candidates, there were 34 female contestants in the fray which constituted 3.1% of the total, out of which only 2 (5.8%) got elected, which meant a mere 1.7 percent" representation in the 112-member unicameral legislature. But this figure increased in 1986 elections as a total of 70 women candidates contested the polls 4.5 percent of the total contestants (1548) but only two (2.6 percent) could win the election.[30]

Compared to the previous regime, the new democratic system having a mandatory constitutional provision for at least five—percent women participation did not substantially improve the situation. In the general elections of May 1991, out of 1345 candidates for the House of Representatives (Lower House), only 79 candidates (5.87 %) were female. The partywise break up of candidates was as follows: The Nepali Congress had 11 female candidates out of 193, CPN -UML had 9 out of 168, RPPs had 17 out of 301, Minor Left parties had 25 female out of 186 and others had 12 out of 348 candidates. Altogether only eight candidates could get into the House of Representatives, among whom five were from the NC and three from the CPN-UML thus amounting to 3.9 percent. The National Assembly (Upper House), a house of 60 members, had three female members.[31]

30. See Suresh C. Chalise, *Sociology of The Legislative Elite In A Developing Society,* Kathmandu : Nepal Foundation for Advanced Studies, 1995, p. 60.
31. *Ibid.,* p. 62.

Age-wise, the female representation seemed to be quite interesting. All legislators are between 25 and 57 showing that the younger and middle-aged generations belong to the leadership structure if they continue to be active in politics even after their term in parliament. Studies have also shown that most female legislators come from the educated sections of society and represent the middle and lower middle class backgrounds. More than 50 percent national and local level women representatives come from the lower middle class strata in terms of economic status and between 30-40 percent and 10 percent respectively from the middle and the lower middle class backgrounds.

It was interesting to note that most active party members, both female and male, were recruited from the student activist group. Among the women leaders, as majority of them used student life as the preparation phase and some of them came into active contacts with the respective party functionaries and became involved in active politics. A party like the RPP fulfilled its quota, if any, by nominating female members from amongst those who had served as women leaders in various organs of the dismantled partyless regime. Among the twenty-nine members of the party's Central Committee, three are female, two Chhetris and one Yadav from the Terai. Similarly, the NC's Central Committee has three members, all from the Koirala clan and belongs to the Brahmin caste group. The CPN-UML Central Committee has three female members of whom two are Brahmin and one

TABLE 6
Gender Composition of Parties' Central Committee Members

	NC		*UML*		*RPP*		*Others*	
Variables	*No*	*%*	*No*	*%*	*No*	*%*	*No*	*%*
Male	28	90.3	32	91.4	26	89.7	86	90.5
Female	3	9.7	3	8.6	3	10.3	9	9.5
Total	31	100	35	100	29	100	95	100

Total members of parties' Central Committees are broken into male/female groups by authors themselves.

Newar married to a Chhetri who too is a member of the same Committee.

Of the total population of Nepal, 50.1 percent (1991 census) is female. Yet, in decision-making processes, women participation is not only negligible but also formalistic in nature. Its reason could be attributed to both the societal factors and to the lack of women movement from the grass-roots level.

The local picture is not as much analogous to the central one as the local NC leaders tend to come from a variety of family and other backgrounds. However, their former sacrifice and struggle for democracy seemed to play a significant role for furthering the cause of their leadership status. So is the case with the CPN-UML.

In the wake of declining capacity of governance displayed by its two principal adversaries, the RPP leaders, on the other hand, often claim that they are better qualified for providing good governance than the NC and the CPN-UML. Their morale is thus boosted owing to two reasons. First, the NC leaders are usually casual in running the elected government, while the CPN-UML is bent on feeding the people with high dose of populism which in course of time may boomerang. Since the CPN-UML party was in power in a minority government putting its eyes on the mid-term elections which it was planning to hold by advising the King to dissolve the House of Representatives, it was capable of projecting its image of a party whose leaders can take swift and efficient policy decisions. A number of popular decisions were then taken by the CPN-UML government adding some feathers in its cap vis-à-vis other parties. But, from a longer-term perspective, such measures adopted for influencing the outcome of the elections would not be sustainable. Another factor that makes the RPP leaders more confident is that they claim that they are better rulers, serious planners and good executioners of policies because of their long and varied experiences in governance during the partyless regime.

Such a national picture is not evident at the lower level as the local leaders are overshadowed by the domineering role and overwhelming presence of the NC and the CPN-UML leaders. These two plus the breakaway communist group—CPN (ML) have occupied most of the elective posts at the local levels. In some districts, however, the RPP continues to play effective leadership role vis-à-vis the other two parties.

III

POWER, LEGITIMACY, STRENGTHS AND WEAKNESSES OF POLITICAL LEADERS

Sources of legitimacy of either organisations or leaders are varied and renewable on the basis of their performance and flexibility. The Nepali leaders, however, seem to get legitimacy from their past roles as tireless fighters for democracy. Thus, historical legitimacy has become one of the primary factors for their long sustenance in today's politics. The NC leaders in particular often advance it as the greatest source of continuity of legitimacy because of their, in their opinion, long-sufferings and involvement in the anti-Rana and anti-Pacnhayat movements. Once Krishna Prasad Bhattarai claimed that so long as the two septuagenarian leaders—G.P. Koirala and himself—remained in the political scene, other leaders would not match them in the NC.

In fact, whether in office and out of office, defeated or victorious in elections, these two leaders continue to do their bidding on personal level and sideline other aspirants. Ganesh Man Singh, the messiah of the 1990 mass movement, continued enjoying his status as the supreme leader (what does it mean in a Democratic Party?) despite his strained relations with the party which he snapped afterwards. Singh did not diminish his role as a strong watchdog against those who often belittled the significance of the spirit of the 1990 movement. G.P.Koirlala's unilateral declaration that Bhattarai would become the next Prime Minister after the election in 1999 without consulting the NC Working Committee and other crucial decisions occasionally taken by them corroborated that the NC politics revolved around these two leaders. If they are together for designating a certain second ranker, then only leadership of government, if not of party, has had been transformed as it happened during Sher Bahadaur Deuba's selection as the leader of the NC parliamentary party and subsequently as Prime Minister during the heyday of political instability after the mid-term poll of 1994. It remained a passing phase because of the transfer of parliamentary party's role to Koirala again and under whose stewardship the NC could win the third general election in 1999 and make Bhattarai the Prime Minister as wished by Koirala. This picture has been considerably changed following the ouster of Bhattarai as Prime Minister after he lost the majority support within his own party and with the keen contest between a second generation leader, Deuba and Koirala, for the leadership of the parliamentary party. Although Koirala defeated Deuba by 26 votes (Koirala 69 and Deuba 43 with one invalid out of 113 members of the House of Representatives), the conventional method of selecting or electing leaders has undergone a change. Now Deuba appears to be zealous of contesting top party posts including that of the Prime Minister thereby indicating that NC politics would not remain the same. What would be the nature of development remains to be seen.

However, the contest by Deuba to the post of the NC's Parliamentary Party Leader was a new development within the NC politics, as by virtue of being the former Prime Minister, he could enhance his status as a leader of the party. Today it has been felt that Deuba , after having once been elevated to the highest office of the country, has become a mini-power centre attracting some aspiring NC members to rally around him in order to be closer to power and status in case he stages a come back in the future. Moreover, the two senior leaders themselves cannot easily write him off because of his former position and legitimacy he has received as a leader. Other second rankers—Ram Chandra Poudel and Shailaja Acharya—

were also made second rankers by the two senior leaders on the grounds of their past records though many others can also stake a claim for such leadership roles. It means that the criteria of ascription partly supported by their past history seemed to have prepared them as prospective leaders for the future. However, how would they be able to assert themselves and succeed the two old leaders depend upon their capacity in the future.

Other parties' leaders also derive legitimacy from the past records. The CPN-UML's past image of being a radical Left party with the objective of changing the feudalistic structure of Nepali society seemed to have added one important feather in its cap. Its past struggle took it to the grassroots level politics with which it could maintain its present status as the second largest party in the country. However, compared to the NC, the CPN-UML leadership is dominated by younger generation leaders who are relatively active, assertive and swift in taking decisions. When the NC starts basking in its past glory, the CPN-UML tends to capitalise each issue on the basis of its often touted " past performance" while in power for nine months thus conjoining the past with the present.

Dominated by the former Panchayat leaders, the RPP seems to be more anxious to prove their prowess on their past records as ministers and legislators. Ridiculing the present party leaders as mismatch for them, they boast of their administrative knack that they learned from the previous regime in governing the country. However, the leaders, many of whom were discredited during the series of coalition formations in the post-1994 mid-term poll, were also perceived as more thorough in their homework and other departmental matters than the NC incumbents. During the 1991-94 parliament, there were only four members from the RPP led by Surya Bahadur Thapa and Lokendra Bahadur Chand, who in fact had better status of being serious and knowledgeable parliamentarians than others.

RPP's legitimacy is therefore hinged more to personalities than to organisation as most top ranking leaders continue to retain their past which in turn also brings with it resources, individual legitimacy and power. Once in power, they could divert resources for renewal of leadership through electoral processes. So positions of power that provide them administrative and financial resources help continue their legitimacy and hence the scramble for power and positions by all variants of leaders is evident.

Other sources of legitimacy were elections held occasionally by the two parties. When partyless politics was much relaxed following the national referendum held in 1980, both the NC and the then CPN (ML) initiated the election procedures for leadership roles at the lower levels. Since the 1990, two national conventions had been held and in the process, lower level competition was evident even for electing representatives to the conventions. The NC's *Maha Samiti* and *Maha Adhibeshan* members who in turn had to elect the central leaders were activated. So was the case with the CPN-UML whose lower level members were in fierce competition while sending delegates to the Sixth Convention held in Nepalgunj in 1998 which eventually led to the split of the party. Competition between the Madhav Nepal -Khadga Oli group and the Bam Dev-C.P. Mainali groups for capturing the senior party posts revealed that even in a communist party such competitive politics determined the leadership structure. It may be recalled here that the parties are needed to fulfil the requirements of the Constitution of the Kingdom of Nepal by having periodic elections within parties. Even for splitting and to be recognised as separate entities, at least forty percent members of the central committee should have joined such splintered groups.[1]

But both the NC and the communist leaders followed the

1. According to Article 113 of the Constitution, parties are required to fulfil these conditions for registration as well as for contesting elections : *(a)* all parties should adhere to the norms of democracy; *(b)* the constitution and rules of the organiations should provide for election of office bearers every five years, *(c)* nay organisation must have secured three percent votes for recognition in the House of Representative and; *(d)* each party must have five percent women representation.

procedure of nomination in the pre-1990 period due to their underground activities. All efforts were geared to achieving their objectives without having to confine themselves to election of leaders. The senior leaders were selected much informally depending on the nature of each party.

Electoral politics also determine the legitimacy of a leader. If certain senior leaders, not those of the first generation, are defeated in parliamentary polls, their chances of being emerged and accepted as apex leaders in government and party are rather reduced. Some others might take the advantage in case the second rankers fail to get into the House of Representatives. However, other sources of legitimacy such as their mass contacts, continuity, mobilising capacity and oratory and popularity on a country-wise basis may compensate electoral setbacks. Constituency politics alone does not prepare a leader of any organisation because in the existing parliamentary set up, a party member can contest elections from any constituency of the country. The former Prime Minister, K P. Bhattarai, after having suffered two electoral setbacks in the capital, won the election from one of the Tarai constituencies in the Parsha district. So for any prospective leader, he should either have national stature or should be fully backed by the party machinery. Other parties' leaders are also doing the same, depending on the resources, popularity and support of the party. So for some, one electoral setback alone would not decide his political future, though for many, such reverses might prove disaster.

Finally, among the new sources of legitimacy at the local level, a person's involvement in local social activities accrues benefits to his constituency or to the district and continue to retain his legitimacy. If some leaders are involved in social welfare activities, rich dividends would be paid to them afterwards in addition to enhancing their political image both symbolically and practically. But the trends of being involved in such social works are limited because most feel that after having been denied any political post to them or defeat in the elections would turn them into political nonentity. Nepal's track record of social service activities carried out by politicians is rare thus driving the politicians at all levels to stick to the conventional route—favour of senior leaders-to status and power. Politics of nomination and path of selectorate therefore become much more significant for them.

Responsibility and Performance

Leaders' responsibilities and performances are always subject to public scrutiny. Symbolically, the central leaders represent the nation, which indirectly put them in interactive roles with the international community also. Their overall leadership roles would be a test case in relation to state-craft. By virtue of being politicians, they have to perform in relation to government regardless of their non-involvement in the governmental processes and functions. So one of the crucial tests of any leader is his role as an interactive leader. If he were in government, statecraft would be such a test case, if not other aspects of legitimacy would be paramount. Similarly, honesty and integrity with which leaders can make good or bad judgements become crucial. Lack of proper judgement in allowing MPs to import luxurious vehicles tax free triggering off widespread condemnation and denunciation from the public in general (nicknaming it as a "Pajero Culture") was a serious miscalculation of most leaders irrespective of parties. All, except a few members and leaders, transcending parties, were unanimous in purchasing such vehicles. Whatever the rationale offered by them, it was generally felt that members of parliament were perceived as rulers, not as representatives of the poor people of Nepal.

The manner in which the politicians are behaving under the present democratic dispensation portrays to the public that their motivation has changed. In the past, they were preoccupied with the politics of survival but today, their survival instinct has been generally transformed into an earning instinct giving rise to doubt in the minds of the people that democracy is only for them, not for the poor sections of the electorate. How the vital issues of public concerns are on the sidelines or are overshadowed by the callous behaviours of leaders could be observed. Not a single decision that can bring about a qualitative change in public life has been addressed during the ten-years' exercises. Institutions are crumbling due to over politicisation and partisan spirit but no parties' leaders seem to be giving serious thought to such issues. Although democratic process has made the electorate more conscious, the leaders have invariably paid short shrift to "democratising democracy". All these aspects covering both local and central levels would be empirically tested in the coming section of this study.

The restoration of multiparty democracy could be considered, at least in theoretical level, as a departure from ascriptive to achievement criteria in emergence of political leaders. The leadership of political parties at both central and local levels are generally entrusted to those persons who have long served for and contributed to their respective parties. People's elected representatives also constitute the leadership of the local and central government. However, it does not mean that the selection of leadership on ascription basis is completely absent in real politics. It is continuing to influence back door or lateral entries through political manipulation. Some argued that the 1990 mass movement brought about changes in political regime but not in the behaviours of political leaders. The domination of power structure by single caste group is a case of unchanged pattern. But it would be a sweeping observation to generalise as other criteria are also simultaneously emerging.

Strength and Weakness

Any discourse on leadership of Nepal would be incomplete unless we bring forth the issues that have had been providing strengths to leaders. First, historically, they (leaders) had been able to change the regimes twice-in 1951 when they successfully transformed the 104-year old family oligarchy of the native Ranas, and in 1990 when all the parties united for dismantling the partyless regime. Their long struggle and sufferings paid off eventually. How the parties leaders were together during and after the movement has been demonstrated by the united effort for making the present Constitution of the Kingdom of

Nepal that changed the status of the Nepalis from subject to sovereign people (from *Praja* to citizen). Although many people now think it as a mere formality because of the diminutive roles of political leaders during the ten-year exercises, major parties are committed to the political processes despite some contradictory signals the communists give from time to time. Nevertheless, since the main stream parties have already tasted power under the present dispensation and are likely to alternate roles from opposition to governing parties and vice versa in the future, the system seems to have withstood the worst phase. Now another phase has just begun for fresh assessment and introspection of the failures of parties and leaders to whom the people are not kind. Such a positive side of the emerging leadership role has also been corroborated by the interviews conducted at the local level. Most of the local leaders said that they are committed to the system.

Second, local leaders are of the opinion that their first priority is to engage themselves in development of their villages and districts and have nothing to do with such issues and events as are occasionally whipped up by the interested parties and leaders. So development is their major preoccupation without which their leadership roles would be seriously undermined. In local and even national elections local issues therefore dominate the electoral politics to which no leaders of parties can ignore.

Third, during the first general election held under the present Constitution in 1991 for electing the representatives to the House of Representatives, issues concerning Indo-Nepal relations particularly relating them to *Rashtrabad* (nationalism) were focused for garnering vote, but now such issues, despite being important, do not attract the people as before. The people, in large, have learnt issues blown up by the interested parties and are not misguided. On the contrary, people vote those leaders who, in their opinion, can fulfil their basic needs —water, health, education, road and employment etc. Political parties' leaders, both at the local and central levels, are expected to be more local than national despite the legislative duties assigned to the members of parliament. Although it appears to be local and even parochial, it is increasingly becoming a source of constant vigilance on the side of the electorate because they evaluate their representatives on the basis of developmental activities they carry out and the contacts they maintain with their voters.

Fourth, political leaders in general are not dogmatic or rigid for interacting with one another. Major decisions have been taken by the coalition government in 1996-97 with the help of the main opposition party—the CPN-UML. Trade and Transit agreement, conclusion of the Mahakali Treaty were accomplished in an atmosphere of understanding. Though these developments were linked to the splits of the two parties —the CPN-UML and the RPP, personality factors seemed to precipitate the split than any other issues. Compared to any other South Asian countries, inter-party relations debunk the overall picture drawn against the leaders of major parties. At the local level too, coalition politics seem to be working quite well in recent years. In many district and village committees, different parties work together forming local coalitions for carrying out developmental works. Building coalitions from the below would definitely help develop a coalition culture at the central level because in a multi-party set up where party splits take place regularly, such coalition culture is a necessary condition for the successful working of democracy.

Fifth, the main factor giving strength to party leaders are the unifying political ideology to which each party, barring the extra-systemic Maoists, is committed. Liberal democracy, despite being denigrated as a Western import and bourgeois in nature, it has demonstrated its integrationist role over the years. Even when the radical groups of the Communist Party of Nepal went on advancing the idea of violent Maoist type revolution from time to time, they seemed to be gradually being absorbed into the plurality of political parties. In 1990, all these groups were together for ending the partyless regime. So given the Nepali reality, it seems that the major parties have no other options but to continue the present multiparty framework, however, with their own respective developmental agendas for the country.

Sixth, a political party like the NC continues to be plagued by intra-party groupism formed along the two major personalities—G.P. Koirala and K.P. Bhattarai. But the NC has avoided splits due to flexibility occasionally displayed by them during the crisis. Other leaders accordingly adjust themselves to the changing lines. Local leaders are too divided over the personality issue but they soon compromise. Some of the leaders who were accused of inflicting damage to party candidates during the general elections have been generally pardoned in order to avoid animosity thus making the NC a loose organisation. Such a situation does not exist in the CPN-UML in view of its relatively stringent party discipline. The RPP, like the NC, continues to be loose in taking any disciplinary action unless its members reach a nadir for splitting the party. Since the RPP is a party of personalities rather than of cadres or masses, it seems to provide a long rope for its members.

Finally, our field surveys conducted in three districts suggest that political leaders at the local level are being prepared indigenously. Their socialisation process is more relevant for the locales of the country and in the intended direction of democratisation. People judge their local leaders and members of parliament on the basis of their commitment to the local interest besides giving attention to their national issues. Now highly personalised party structure at the central level (especially of the NC) is likely to be challenged by the upcoming generation of leaders after sometime. The central leaders who have been basking in their past deeds would no longer be able to do so in the future in view of a new democratic orientation being received by the local leaders.

Weaknesses of leaders are related to their backgrounds, organisational structures, and motivation. Our discourse on strengths can also reveal weaknesses. From what socio-political and economic backgrounds the leaders come and what new values they have internalised become significant. Leaders generally are weak when they make departures from core values to which they had all along been committed. Political expediency and value-free approach to any event and issue make the leaders more compromising as did the party leaders in the post-1990 period. Compared to the central level, local leaders are still better disciplined and articulated. However, acknowledging their leaders past records and leadership qualities, the local leaders continue to show their deference to their central leaders despite having seen erosion in the popularity of their senior leaders.

So political leaders are yet to pass through internal crises in view of their highly centralised structure. Few individual leaders of the NC still dominate the party as if it is their fief. And no leaders of other generations can challenge this inherited status making the leadership role more personalised. Compared to the NC, the CPN-UML has better inner party democracy but the personality factors which loom large has always been divisive. When party leaders fail to be flexible or are adrift due to various intervening factors—ambition, manipulation from outside, money etc.—, chances of breaking homogeneity are always great. But lack of assertiveness on the part of NC second and other rankers, the two apex leaders have managed to run the party according to styles befitting their backgrounds.

Let us look at the social and economic background of the communist parties of Nepal. The Marxist-movement in Nepal is confined to middle and lower middle class or/and petit bourgeoisie classes of the society. If the soul of Marxism is the most disadvantaged class of society which is constituted in Nepal by the "exploited class composed of landless, lower middle level peasants, artisans, rikshaw-pullers, small traders and entrepreneurs and labourers", the Nepali Marxist movement has become an exclusive domain of the former categories (middle and lower middle classes).[2] The composition of leadership of the CPN-UML and other groups shows such a paradox. The middle class values further

2. See Lok Krishna Bhattarai, "Kamyunist Andolanma Sahi Pakshyako Utham" (Upliftment of Real Section), *Kantipur Daily*, December 1, 1999.

reinforced by the emergent trends of globalisation and consumerism have been further enforced making these parties to be less relevant to the cause of the poor sections of society.

The NC is not different from the CPN-UML and is dominated by the middle and lower middle classes. Middle class dominates the Central Working Committee and other local committees which are predominantly caste biased. Professionals joining the party get less priority as the personal, family and other parochial considerations seem to determine the composition patterns. So in Nepal, leadership in the strict sense of the term, is still an ascribed phenomenon because of the pervasive influence of caste, family and personal influence of senior leaders.

The rise of consumerist culture that motivates the leaders to be more ostentatious in their life styles is believed to have degraded their stature. All leaders have invariably surpassed the former *panchas* for converting themselves into members of a new class regardless of the poor people they represent creating a hiatus between them and the people. The leaders and political elites, in general, have approached politics as a profession, an earning source which, in turn, becomes a resource for winning elections and for perpetuating positions of power. It has thus created a nexus between the politicians and illegitimate sources of income. Money power also brings along with it the muscle power for furthering the prospects of electoral gains.

Political parties' leaders are increasingly becoming hostages to the providers of funds mobilised from a variety of sources. The major parties when they are in government make maximum use of governmental channels for resource mobilisation. And those who allegedly provide part of such earnings to the party leaders continue to be in government contrary to their public image. If the NC seems to face such a cruel dilemma of making them as both assets and liabilities, the CPN (UML) has institutionalised corruption for generating funds for the party. All political appointees and members of parliament and others who earn by virtue of being the role incumbents are required to pay part of such earnings to the party. From one pint of view, it appears as a genuine way of collecting fund, from another angle, it can be called an institutionalised corruption as people aspiring for various jobs would be encouraged to pay in commensurate with the money they get.

Do the Nepali leaders scramble for posts and even for joining politics owing to economic insecurity or are they both the symptoms and diseases of the ideologically debased politics? As many of them make politics as an exclusive profession, they are apparently motivated by a psyche of get-rich quick for both livelihood as well as for continuing in the present electoral politics which is increasingly becoming expensive and competitive. Parties' leaders who are popular at the lower levels cannot "extend their influence beyond a particular area, group or community"[3] if they lack the funds. But today's trend is rather alarming inasmuch as all categories of leaders seem to be indulgent in amassing wealth for both running parties and personal reasons.

Another weakness of leaders is to allow personalised groupism within a party. Personalised groupism tends to use a leader or leaders for enhancing the interests of the members of that group as in their strategic thinking, they would be left aside without the patronage and shelter of a leader. All parties -particularly the NC and the CPN (UML)-are plagued by it. While distributing patronage, the members of the group are needed to be duly recognised and accommodated in various posts either in government or in an organisation. The apex leaders sometimes are hostages to such placatory politics having extensive effects on the lower levels. Any party has its own crisis management techniques, if not mechanisms, which vary from party to party. The NC is peculiarly characterised by a high degree of personalised groupism, often at the cost of its credibility and popularity.

---

3. In the 1950s also, problems of economic insecurity seemed to dominate those who tried to make politics as an exclusive profession. If leaders came from other profession—lawyers, professors, doctors, engineers etc.—they did not care much for earnings. For such trends, see Anirudha Gupta, *Politics in Nepal : 1950-60,* Delhi : Kalinga, 1993, p. 221.

On the basis of foregoing resume of strength and weakness of leaders, it can be said that perception, image and reality of leaders are changing. People's perceptions of leaders, which were more or less based on superficiality, are no more so in view of the intermixing trends of intellectual perception, general people's perception and workers' perception. Intellectuals want to see their leaders more innovative, dynamic, clean, visionary and bold who can take decisions and implement them. In absence of these credentials, leaders are subject to criticism. Sometimes, leaders who ought to be perceived as role-model, not only lack all of the above mentioned qualities but also go on adding more negative qualities such as self-centred, callous, short-sighted and whimsical as if such leaders take the people for granted. In absence of a strong civil society movement, political leaders go berserk as no other leaders and parties have the courage to take them to task for their wrongful actions and utterances. Such a sense of self- righteousness seems to be both outlandish and disastrous for their own parties.

Such intellectual perceptions of leaders have also been shared by parties' workers and other general people, though for party elites, their leaders have some extra-ordinary qualities with which their parties are being managed. However, with the rising consciousness and greater degree of objectivity, parties' elites see their leaders through the same prism as seen by others. Yet, they, as party loyalists, need to be discreet in their regular behaviour. Unless political parties allow inner party democracy to flourish and respect dissent, the prospects of growth of leadership become bleak. In the present situation, however, such a possibility seems to be remote because of the highly personalised, feudalistic and centralised behaviours of leaders who want servile submission of their subordinates rather than their critical opinion before taking any important decision. It, however, needs to be cautioned that not all parties suffer from these undemocratic trends as we have already remarked elsewhere about inner-party democracy in some organisations.

The domination of some old leaders who had never run

parties in an institutionalised manner and who were also temperamentally disposed to make their organisations as "personality parties" never paid any attention to convert them as vibrant democratic institutions. So in a party like the NC, which had undergone vicissitudes in its life, the emergence of second generation of leaders who can both mobilise and attract people towards their personalities, could not be observed. Old leaders' political style and behaviour has now, it seems, been copied by the so-called succeeding generation of leaders, though it is too early to infer any conclusion on their leadership role when they will replace the old leaders. Since the institutionalisation "can be measured on two scales"—degree of autonomy of an organisation and degree of ' systemness',[4] such a phenomenon is almost absent in parties despite all the formal structures remaining intact.

By contrast, the CPN-UML is a party of collective leadership composed of middle-aged generation of leaders. Most senior leaders—members of the Standing Committee—are the products of the underground violent movement of the late 1960s and early '70s and were in various incarnations swinging from one political spectrum into the other both in terms of ideological shifts and tactical lines. Finally, obviously making an objective study of their own past mistakes, they seem to have taken yet another plunge into multiparty politics in 1990. Such a pragmatic approach has indeed paid rich dividends to its leaders by catapulting them into government and opposition and also by showing the party's actual potential as an alternate force in Nepali politics. Yet, the CPN-UML seems to face the dilemma on whether or not the party should fully and permanently be committed to the multiparty system. Conflicting signals that underlie its ultimate objective of reaching a people's democracy (*Janbad*) whatever vague it might be have had given rise to questions about its credibility. But the existing realities at both national and international levels suggest such postures are essential due to its background

4. Angelo Panebianco, *Political Parties : Organization and Power*, London : Cambridge University Press, 1998, p. 55.

and messiah-like image of a revolutionary party. For fear of being discredited by other groups and also for keeping its followers intact, the party leaders cannot at once make a radical departure from its original identity despite its role being graduated into a systemic party which is close to power by virtue of being the main opposition party as well as by its own organisational networks at the local levels.

IV

SOCIAL, ECONOMIC AND POLITICAL BACKGROUND OF LOCAL LEADERS

In democracy, leadership is an outcome of the party's deliberate choice and people's preference. In multiparty competitive system, particularly in the Nepali experience, non-party candidates were almost rejected by the people. So the crucial role of parties has been vindicated by such electoral trends.

However, people's endorsement of the parties' candidates through a elections is a must in multiparty system. At the same time factors such as cultural, social, economic influence the people's choice. It is therefore, well understood that a party tries to maintain the balance amongst different segments of the society while performing one of its major functions i.e. recruitment of political leaders. The more the party leadership is constituted by men/women of different social and economic strata, the more diversified is its social bases. The composition of party leaders in terms of their socio-economic backgrounds is considered as a mirror of the party's social bases. All three major political parties of Nepal- the NC, the CPN-UML and the RPP—can be considered as broad based national parties in view of their reach and wider base. The table 7 on page 73 shows plurality in composition of local level leaders of three major political parties of Nepal.

The survey represents all age groups of 100 respondents and shows the composition of local leaders of each of the three major parties namely the NC, the CPN-UML and the RPP. A majority of them, 56 out of 100, belong to middle aged people.

TABLE 7
Socio-Economic Background of Local Leaders

Variables	*NC(33)*	*UML(44)*	*RPP(17)*	*Others(6)*	*Total(100)*
1. Age					
Young	14	19	1	3	37
Middle	17	24	12	3	56
Old	2	1	4	—	7
2. Education					
Illiterate	2	—	1	—	3
Literate	—	7	—	—	7
School Level	8	18	8	3	37
Higher Level	23	19	8	3	53
3. Class					
Rich	—	—	1	—	1
Middle	19	15	12	2	48
Lower Middle	14	28	4	4	50
Poor	—	1	—	—	1
4. Occupation					
Agriculture	10	11	7	3	31
Business	6	11	5	1	23
Student	12	14	—	2	28
Service	2	2	4	—	8
Teachers	2	4	—	—	6
Others	1	2	1	—	4
5. Sex					
Male	33	44	16	6	99
Female	—	—	1	—	1
6. Caste/Ethnicity					
Hill Castes	15	10	5	3	33
Brahmin	4	12	3	3	22
Chhetri	2	11	1	—	15
Hill Ethnic					
Tarai Plain Group	12	11	6	—	28
Others	—	—	2	—	2

This group dominates the composition of local leadership of all the three parties. 17 out of 33 NC's leaders belonged to this group, followed by 24 in 44 CPN-UML's leaders and 12 in 17 RPP leaders.

A substantial number of young people are coming up in leadership posts. Thus, a new trend seems to be emerging after the restoration of democracy. The bulk of political leadership under the partyless Panchayat regime was mostly dominated by the middle and old age groups.

The old age group is slowly being phased out from local politics in the post-Panchayat time, since this age group has marginal representation (as shown in the table 7), only seven out of 100 local leaders. Only two from the NC, one from the CPN-UML and four from the RPP had come from the old age group in leadership composition of respective parties. Younger age group people are coming up in local leadership because increasing unemployment problem has given rise to them, while opposite may be the case when the parties' patronage distribution functions create relations between politics and younger age group. Despite the debate, youth participation in politics and their prominence in the leadership level is a welcome trend. Around 44 percent of the NC and the CPN-UML's local leaders come from young age group but in the case of RPP, it has poor representation of this group. This indicates that the centrist NC and the leftist CPN-UML are more able to attract the younger generation. Some changes are also appearing in the leadership pattern of the NC and the CPN-UML. A number of opinion surveys[1] conducted in the early 1990s (following the restoration of democracy) found a distinction between the NC and the CPN-UML in terms of choice of the party by the people of different age groups. These surveys found that the younger generation preferred the CPN-UML, whereas the NC had stronghold among the middle and old age groups. The generational differences in party choice are because of the history of these two parties. Being the oldest party of Nepal founded in 1947, the NC had been favoured by the middle and old age people. The CPN-UML is relatively

1. See IIDS, *The Second Parliamentary Election : A Study of Emerging Democratic Process in Nepal,* Kathmandu : IIDS, 1993; POLSAN, *Nepalases Voters : A Survey Report,* Kathmandu : POLSAN, 1991; Ole Borre, S.R. Pandey and C.K. Tiwari, *Nepalase Political Behaviour,* New Delhi : Sterling 1994.

a new party with its origin only in the late '70s. Therefore, it had good influence among the younger age groups. But the generational differences in choice of party between the NC and the CPN-UML is now changing as suggested by the equal representation (in percentage) of young age groups in composition of local leaders of these parties.

Education

In Nepal where half of the total 22 million population is illiterate, educated persons are generally respected by the society. Educational attainment is, therefore, an important factor, if not a prerequisite, for everyone in the society. As an anthropologist has said, "To be educated is a powerful symbol of status."[2]

The educated mass of Nepal has love and hate relations with politics. On the one hand, this class has engineered major political changes in the country beginning with 1950 revolution to the recent 1990 pro-democracy movement, however, on the other hand, at the personal level, the educated persons seem reluctant to join politics and develop their career and profession in politics. There is a popular saying that in Nepal the first class degree holders receive lucrative jobs abroad; the second class adjusts to bureaucracy and other jobs within the country; and the third class join politics. This may be considered as one of the reasons behind the poor quality of politics and leadership in Nepal. It does not mean that the educated mass of Nepal is less politicised. Most of them were actively involved in opposition politics against the regime, particularly during the past panchayat regime.

After the 1960 royal coup, the NC relied heavily on the support of the educated middle class. It enlisted new cadre, most of them coming from educational institutions which were excessively politicized during the panchayat time. *The Nepal Vidyarthi Sangh* (NVS), a pro-Congress student wing founded in 1970, had intensified its activities by spreading its local branches in all campuses and schools in most districts. The

2. Dor Bahadur Bista, *"Fatalism and Development : Nepal's Struggle for Modernization"*, Calcutta : Orient Longman, 1991, p. 5.

associations of pro—Congress university and school teachers had also their own local units in their respective field -, campuses and schools across the country.

The influence of NC in educational institutions had a chain of multiple effects in enlarging its support bases among the educated people. It gradually extended its influence in bureaucracy, semi-government corporations and professional organizations resulting in the embarrassment of the government during the elections of four graduate representatives from amongst the graduates of the country. In the two graduate elections held in 1967 and 1971, the anti-regime dissidents won the election showing that the intelligentsia of the country was not at all happy with the partyless regime led by the King. In addition to the near-unanimity among the anti-panchayat candidates for (a) adult franchise, (b) relaxation in fundamental rights, (c) release of political prisoners, and (d) grant of amnesty to those living in India as oppositionists. Some hard-core critics were more vociferous in demanding the revival of political parties to which the government objected to having crossed the limits of the Constitution and took repressive measures depriving them opportunities for getting into the legislature. In 1971, all the dissidents won the election but later, one of them was expelled from the legislature on the grounds of his nonconformist behaviour during and after the election.[3] Eventually, this constituency was removed by the second amendment to the constitution in 1975.

Most educated people had been socialized in politics during their student life. Their inclination with certain political values and affiliation with particular political party that built up during the student life remained somehow alive after they entered their own occupation and profession. Consequently, there were thousands of sympathizers of the NC and the Communist groups in governmental and semi-governmental offices. The panchayat by contrast represented only marginally the country's intelligentsia which was clearly manifested in

3. See Lok Raj Baral, *Oppositional Politics in Nepal,* Delhi : Abhinav, 1977, pp. 136-44.

various graduate elections and later during the national referendum ordered by King Birendra for soliciting the mandate for continuing the then existing system with reforms or for reviving the multiparty system. In fact, the declaration of national referendum was the consequence of the country-wide student movement launched on the pretext of protesting against the hanging of zulfikar Ali Bhutto, the dismissed prime minister of Pakistan in 1979. Bhutto was dislodged in the military coup staged by ZiaulHaq, Bhutto's own Chief of the Army Staff, and put to death for the alleged charges of murder of a politician of Pakistan.[4]

Moreover, the politicization of educational institutions led to producing a new generation of parties' activists from the educated people who were socialized in politics during their student life and those who were projected as student leaders later used to join political parties. Most NC's second generation leaders and also its district level leaders are product of post-1960 politics. They started their political career as activists of the NVS. The growth of education contributed to generating the NC cadre from the new generation of educated people.

The relationship between the growth of the educational institutions and the party building was more tied up in the case of the Communist Party of Nepal, Marxist-Leninist (now UML and its splinter group which borrowed original name, the ML). While building its support bases, the ML had made the educational institutions as the sites of recruitment of party members because of two reasons. First, it was relatively safe and convenient to carry out underground activities through the profession of teaching. Most hard core activists in the ML rank and file including the present central and district leaders spread the party's clandestine activities through school teachers. The second advantage that the ML had taken was its popularity within the teaching community. The pro-ML teachers used to socialize during their student days from the secondary level which had naturally impacted in the

4. See for detail, Lok Raj Baral, *Nepal's Politics of Referendum : A Study of Groups, Personalities and Trends,* Delhi : Vikas, 1983.

environment of higher education and also spreading the party's student wing in many parts of the country in short time.

The more the people are educated the more greater would be the prospect for democracy and political parties.[5] The result of all the four seats of the graduates' constituency elections in the panchayat legislature went in favour of the Congress and Communist backed candidates in all times until this provision itself was abolished since 1975. The pro-Congress and the pro-Communist student groups had maintained their domination as major threats to the regime. Student unions which were treated as anti-regime, used to draw attention of the government as they were considered as the representatives of the outlawed political parties. Other professional organizations were also perceived as pro-parties regardless of the regime's mobilization strategy of creating a single organization befitting the "partyless" spirit of the regime.

How student groups had great impact on changing the course of political development could be observed from time to time. The student agitation that went on for six weeks in April-May 1979 affecting 40 out of 75 districts forced King Birendra to declare a referendum in May 1979. The referendum, held a year later, favoured the status quo by a margin of 10 percent votes. The multiparty side scored high in the areas where the facility of education, transportation, communication, and urbanization was available, while showing poor performance in the underdeveloped and least developed areas. Votes for multi-party side was only 28.9% in 15 mountain districts and 48.8 per cent in 37 hill districts whereas the figure was 55% in 18 plain districts and 66% in five inner Tarai districts.[6] Nevertheless the victory of the panchayat in the referendum did not stop the politicization process against the establishment. It went on developing beyond the educational institutions since the reformed

5. For the impact of educational growth in democracy movements in Nepal, see Dipak Raj Pant, "Higher Education and Liberal Values in Nepal", *European Bulletin of Himaliayan Researh,* No. 9, 1995.
6. Rishikesh Shaha, *Politics in Nepal: 1980-1991,* New Delhi: Manohar, 1993, pp. 70-71.

panchayat system failed in integrating its own supporters. This triggered off more contradictions and paranoia within the regime suggesting that the regime's individualistic orientation and legal provisions did not go along with the broadbased electoral politics. On the one hand, attempts were made to protect the partyless spirit and royal leadership, the façade of political liberalization was to be demonstrated for its popular legitimacy on the other.

Unlike the domination of just literate and low level educated persons in leadership structure in the past under the panchayat regime, the post-1990 democratic period has shown that more educated persons seem to be taking up leadership of the party and the country at different levels. Out of 100 local leaders sampled for this study, 53 have higher-level educational background. 70 percent of NC's 33 local leaders are highly educated. The local leadership of the CPN-UML is constituted by both the higher level and school level certificate holders. The representation of people from literate and illiterate categories is very nominal at the leadership hierarchy. This reveals the fact that there is a strong positive correlation between education and leadership development. An Anthropologist has rightly observed the formation of political leadership in Nepal and states: "The English education and the money power will play more important role than the hierarchical caste structure of Nepali society."[7]

Class

The leadership of the NC and the CPN-UML is pre-dominated by the middle class people. The economic position of the RPP leadership is relatively better off since it was formed by the former rulers. A substantial number of Congress and Communist leaders had come from the rich and feudal backgrounds since the inception of the parties. But most

7. Dilli Ram Dahal, "Nepal's Governing Elite : Their composition and Role in Constituting the State", in Dhruba Kumar, ed., *Domestic Conflicts and Crisis of Governability in Nepal,* Kathmandu : Centre for Nepal and Asian Studies, 2000.

of them left the parties after the introduction of the partyless Panchayat System through a royal coup in December 1960, hence the leadership of the NC and communist parties were confined to the people of educated middle class. It reveals the fact that the rich as well as poor have a tendency to associate themselves with the establishment and not with the opposition. The roles of the NC and the CPN-UML have changed from an opposition to that of the rulers and vice versa but, interestingly, both groups retain their middle class character.

The RPP leadership is mainly constituted by those people who have relatively better economic status than their Congress and Communist counterparts. It has its own antecedents as most leaders were former panchayat leaders who had long experience of running the country in different capacities. Conceivably, their own family backgrounds and better economic positions plus the uninterrupted opportunities got by them made them adept in electioneering. Since they continue to contest elections from their own well nurtured constituencies since the panchayat days, they have had certain edge over their party rivals.

Most panchayat posts from village to national levels were held by the high caste groups and by the well to do families.[8] Apart from close correlation between high caste status, control

8. For leadership pattern in local level during partyless Panchayat System, see L.S. Baral, "The First Panchayat Elections in Nepal, 1962-63 : The Emergence of A New Political Generation", *International Studies,* Vol. 12, January-December 1973; Lok Raj Baral, *Village Politics and Development : A Study of Three Village Panchayat* (Unpublished Memo), Kathmandu : CNAS/TU, 1978; "Nepal : Local Politics and Some Trends of Social Change", *Indian Journal of Nepalese Studies,* Vol. 1, July-December 1987, pp. 31-40; Lionel Caplan, *Administration and Politics in a Nepalese Town : The Study of a District Capital and its environs,* London : Oxford University Press, 1975; Pashupati Shamsher Rana and Mohammad Mohsin, *A Study Report on the Pattern of Emerging Leadership in Panchayets,* Kathmandu : CEDA/TU, 1967; R.S. Chauhan, *The Political Development in Nepal 1950-70 : Conflict Between Tradition and Modernity,* New Delhi : Associated Publishing House, 1971; Abullaish, *Effectiveness of Local Leadership for Change and*

of land, and ruling elite structure, a person needed to cultivate his family ties and kinship, and other connections with the high ranking post holders in administrative and political structures of the country. Such a system of patron-client relations in elite formation worked effectively[9] in the absence of party politics and also lack of adult franchise before the 1980 referendum. The panchayat system reinforced the tradition of *Hukumi Raj* (rule by peremptory command), so the closer to the palace the more prospect if one is to be in power. In addition to the state's bureaucratic mechanism, the palace had its own vertical channels of him/her,—the palace secretariat at the top, King's nominees Zonal Commissioner, and Chief District Officer accountable to Zonal Commissioner, which not only guarded the King's traditional power of Hukumi Raj, but also actively intervened in politics granting patronage to the people of their favour to be recruited in the ruling elite structure. In average, the portrait of the panchayat ruling elites, from village chairman to Prime Minister, could be presented in these words: middle or old aged people having just literate or low level education (around 40 % member of last National Panchayat had higher level education); hill born,

---

Transformation of Rural Society, Kathmandu : CEDA/TU, 1982. For the pattern of high ranking Panchayat leaders see Lok Raj Baral, *Pattern of Representation in the National Panchayat of Nepal,* Kathmandu : INAS/TU, 1975; Rishikesh Shaha, "The Nepalese Ministerial Elite Since 1960 : Change and Continuity of the Political Elite" *The Nepalese Elite,* Banaras : Center for the Study of Nepal 1982; Satyendra Tripathi, "Political Elite and Their Strategies in Nepal", *The Nepalese Elite,* op.cit. S.C. Chalise, "The Social Background of Legislative Elite in Nepal, 1986", *Indian Journal of Nepalese Politics,* Vol. 1., July-December 1987, pp. 81-92.

9. Bengt-Erik Borgrstrom had first applied the pattron-client model in assessing Nepali politics and leadership in micro levl. Later, Rishikesh Shaha applied this model while making an indepth analysis of the elite formation in Nepal and located the hierarchical position of top ranking political elites during the Panchayat time. See Bengt-Erik Borgstrom, *The Patron and the Panca : Village Values and Panchayat Democracy in Nepal,* New Delhi : Vikash Publishing House, 1980; Rishikesh Shaha, *Essays in the Practice of Government in Nepal,* New Delhi : Manohar Publications, 1982.

high caste and wealthy; decedents of traditionally *Thalu* family; and having strong family and kinship ties with the people of higher echelon in power structure of the country. In sum, the political system and political process under panchayat system was highly in favour of maintaining status quo in elite structure nevertheless some notable change appeared in favour of traditionally unprivileged sections of the people as an impact of introducing direct elections in post-1980 referendum period.[10]

The class composition of 100 local leaders, selected for this study, is not identified by considering their financial assets i.e. land, house, vehicles and others. It is based on the personal observation and impression of field surveyers about the respondents and respondents' own submission. The tabulated data on class suggests that almost all-local leaders have come from middle and lower middle class backgrounds. The representation of middle class in the RPP leadership is higher (71 percent) than those of the NC and the CPN-UML. Nevertheless, a number of middle class people (that is 19 and 58 percent) is more than the lower class in total 33 NC local leaders. In the CPN-UML, the lower middle class has greater representation of 64 percent than that of the middle class constituting its local leadership. Though this party presents itself as the vanguard of poor, the data suggest otherwise as only one person from the poor group background is represented in its leadership composition. It is interesting that

10. Some leading analysists of Nepali politics observed that the introduction of adult franchise but without the system of party competition in the post-referendum period led to the emergence of ethnic and communal politics in electoral behaviours. By the use of ethnic, caste and community cards, a number of previously diadvantaged groups i.e. hill and plain tribes and plain middle caste like Yadav succeded in increasing their numbers in National Panchayat. See Baral, *Nepal's Politics of Referendum, op.cit.* and his "The First Panchayat General Election in Nepal", *The Nepalese Journal of Political Science,* Vol. VI, No. 2, December 1981; Shaha, *Politics in Nepal 1980-91,* op.cit.; Harka Gurung, "Sociology of Elections in Nepal, 1959-1981" *Asian Survey,* Vol. XXIV, No. 3, March 1982, pp. 304-14.

the people from both the rich and poor economic backgrounds are almost absent in leadership structure at the local level throughout the sampled districts.

Occupation

In response to a question—what was your main occupation before you took politics as a profession?—Many respondents identified one of the three major occupations—agriculture, student and business. 31 out of 100 said they come from agricultural occupation. This is quite surprising that more than 80 percent of the Nepali population work in the agriculture sector. Nearly one-fourth local leaders come from business community which is bigger than the real size and strength of this community vis-à-vis political leadership. This, however, gives a finding that the middle and the lower middle classes are dominant in the local politics and leadership. The NC and the CPN-UML have a commonality that the number of people who switched from student life into politics is higher in the composition of total numbers of local leaders of these two respective parties. One-third local leaders of these parties identified themselves as student before they entered into active politics. It reveals that many NC and CPN-UML local leaders have been politically socialised and recruited during their student life. Since the rank and file of the ML, which became CPN-UML after its unification with the Marxist faction, operated their underground politics as school teachers during the panchayat period. Therefore, it is widely assumed that a large number of its local leaders come from teaching profession. However, the data here do not support this hypothesis. Only few numbers from teaching and other occupations form the local leadership of the CPN-UML. The aggregate data of all 100 respondents and their party-wise breakdown show that the people of agriculture, student and business occupations primarily dominate the local leadership except the RPP composition.

The party-wise breakdown of occupational background follows this trend. Among the NCs 33 local leaders, leaders from the student background are 12, followed by agricultural occupation group 10, business community six, teacher two, breaucracy two and other one. The occupational composition of 44 CPN-UML local leaders is as follows: student 14, peasant 11, businessmen 11, teachers four, service two and others two. The occupational composition of the RPP leaders is somewhat different from those of the NC and the CPN-UML. Its 17 local leaders come from these backgrounds—peasant seven, businessmen five, bureaucracy four and others one. Representation from student community and teaching profession is almost nil in the RPP local leadership structure.

Gender

The representation of only one female in sampled hundred local leaders shows the underrepresented position of women in politics and in leadership role of Nepal. This figure is lower than six percent women representation in the present 205-member House of Representatives but it corresponds to 0.7 percent women elected from amongst several hundred members of 75 District Development Committees. In replying to the question—why the Nepali women never played a role of governing elite in Nepal as of now? An observer said, "it is the culture that excluded Nepali women for becoming governing elites in Nepali society throughout history."[11] The Constitution of the Kingdom of Nepal,1990 locates the position of women as one of the disadvantaged sections of society deserving special treatment from the state in the limited areas such as education, health and employment. In politics, the Constitution provides for reservation of five percent women in total candidates of each competing party for parliamentary elections and other five percent women representation in 60 member National Assembly. The Local Government Act- 1998 provides one-fourth seat reservation for women in 5- member Ward Committee of each village, the lowest elected body, in addition to another mandatory provision that at least one woman must be nominated as the member of each Village Development Committee and District Development

11. Dahal, *Op.Cit.*, p. 5.

Committee.[12] The reservation for women representation in leadership position is negligible in comparison to reservation of one-third seats in India. Indeed, women's representation hardly exceeds the reserved seat. The three major political parties—the NC, the CPN-UML and the RPP—recently introduced a provision in their own respective party constitutions that 10 percent of the total members of the party' executive committees at all levels must be women. But this provision is seldom followed by local leaders of these parties. In fact, the women or gender component has hardly been considered as an important variable in party building activities and in election strategies. Therefore, the under-representation of women in leadership position shows the continued social disparity in the country's politics.

Caste/Ethnicity

The question of unequal distribution of power has arisen much strikingly from the caste/ethnic angles. The high hill caste groups, Brahmin and Chhetri , constitute 33 percent in total population of Nepal but they have occupied most posts and positions in power structure. Among the 100 local leaders selected for this study, 55 have come from Brahmin—Chhetri caste groups. This figure corresponds to national picture in leadership position in Caste/ethnic terms. Domination of the high hill caste groups in composition of political leadership at national and local levels reflects their pre-eminence in social, economic, administrative and political structures of the country.

Though caste domination and discrimination has been legally abolished since Nepal entered into modern phase by the mid-20th century, the domination of the hill high caste groups has been retained by the two principal factors: one is the ascendancy of Brahmin and Chhetri in acquiring new sources of power i.e. education, communication and modernisation and the other one is the continued trend of social disparity based on traditional ethos of the past. In the

12. See *National Gender Analysis on Elected and Nominated Women Ward Representatives*, Kathmandu : UNDP, 1998.

given historical context, the domination of the high hill caste groups over other ethnic communities in Nepali politics remains unchanged irrespective of the structural change in political system i.e. from partyless Panchayat system into multiparty democracy because the multiparty system is as much caste-bound as the previous partyless regime.

The ethnic upsurge against Brahmin-Chhetri domination, popularly known as *Janjati Abhiyan*, is increasingly becoming evident in the post-1990 political developments. The Constitution of the Kingdom Nepal,1990 acknowledges cultural pluralism but it rejects ethnopolitics imposing restriction on forming political parties on the basis of religion, language, community and region. The popular rejection of narrowly confined ethnopolitics has been manifested time and again. Some ethnic and region- based parties manage to contest the elections despite legal restrictions, but they have failed to win a single seat, except the Nepal Sadbhawana Party (NSP), a Tarai-based regional party, showed its presence with its few seats in the parliament. The rejection of ethnic party by the moter but the rise of *Janjati Abhiyan* seems self-contradictory. However, it suggests that the political parties are managing the problems of balancing caste/ethnic components in leadership structure at local levels.

In the sampled multi-constituency districts, all the three major political parties—the NC, the CPN-UML and the RPP—had selected candidates for parliamentary elections from the two major communities of respective districts i.e. Brahmin/ Chhteri and Rai-Limbu in Ilam district and migrant hill caste and Tarai people in Dhanusha. It indicates that political parties consider social division in selecting their local as well national leaders, since voters generally prefer candidates of their own caste/community and neighbourhood groups than to others from distant areas. Parties, therefore, usually recruit their own local leaders from locally dominated caste/ethnic groups. This pattern is reflected in district-wise breakdowns of sampled 100 local leaders (Ilam-34, Dhanusha-34 and Dadeldhura-32). In Ilam district, where Rai-Limbu community constitutes majority group, they represent 38 percent out of the 34 local leaders selected from this district. The case of Dhanusha is extreme that 82 percent among the sampled 34 local leaders is formed by *Madhesi* community.

Dadeldhura is an exception where one-forth of district population is constituted by the untouchable caste but all 32 sampled leaders belong to Brahmin and Chhetri. The total exclusion of the untouchable caste in leadership structure is a national phenomenon. The party-wise breakdown of 100 sampled local leaders establishes the fact that political parties have more or less integrated the minority communities into the leadership structure at the local level though 58 percent of the NC local leaders have come from the hill high caste Brahmin and Chhetri. The *Madhise* community constitutes one third of its total local leaders. The RPP local leadership pattern is more or less similar to that of the NC except its accommodation of two Muslims (other category in the table) but not by the NC and the CPN-UML. The CPN-UML has given fair representation, as one-fourth from each of the Hill Ethnic Group and Tarai caste group is in its local leadership. In sum, the people from hill caste groups, middle aged, higher level educated groups, lower middle class status and agricultural occupation form the core local leadership.

Family background of Local Leaders

The local leaders of Nepal have come from six different types of family backgrounds. They are: *Thalu, Mahajan,* priest, politicians, service holders and commoner. *Thalu* refers to privileged family who enjoyed the title of *Mukhiya, Jimmawal, Talukdar, Jamindar and Khandaniya* in the past. *Mahajan* is a title given to the rich person, especially during the Rana period. *Thalu, Mahajan* and priest have traditionally influenced and controlled the social behaviour and economic life of the country, for they had proximity to politics. Their influences have now declined considerably with the increasing impact of modernisation. By the mid-20th century, politicians and bureaucrats emerged as the influential groups sharing the state power with traditional elites. So the local leaders of the given six family backgrounds can be broadly classified into two

TABLE 8
Sources of Power of Local Leaders

Variables	*NC(33)*	*UML(44)*	*RPP(17)*	*Others(6)*	*Total(100)*
1. Family Background					
Thalu	3	2	3	—	8
Mahajan	5	2	6	—	13
Priest	3	4	—	—	7
Politicians	6	4	—	2	12
Service	3	9	3	—	15
Commoner	13	23	5	4	45
2. Relative in Power Structure					
No	13	27	7	5	52
Yes, (where)	*20*	*17*	*10*	*1*	*48*
Party	9	6	3	—	18
Elected Body	3	6	1	—	10
Bureaucracy/Others	8	5	6	1	20
3. Personal Capabilities					
Family background	7	8	5	2	22
Economic position	1	—	—	—	1
Caste/ethnic factor	2	1	2	—	5
Personality	13	18	15	2	48
Sacrifice	9	14	2	1	26
Continuity	19	27	4	3	53
Contribution to social reform	6	12	9	5	32
Involvement in *Jan Andolan*	11	5	—	—	16
Active in elections	8	6	—	—	14
Others	4	5	—	4	13
4. Internal Support from:					
Party high commands	10	—	1	—	11
Central level leaders	5	—	1	—	6
District level leaders	14	7	10	3	34
Party workers	27	41	13	5	86
Factions	5	—	3	1	9
Others	2	5	2	5	14
5. Social Affiliation with Organisations					
No	8	25	7	2	42
Yes, (types)	*25*	*19*	*10*	*4*	*58*
Cultural/religious	3	1	2	—	6
Education/Health	5	6	4	—	15
Development	1	4	1	3	9
Social Service	6	—	—	—	6
Professional	3	2	2	1	8
Human Rights	1	2	—	—	3
General	6	4	1	—	11

categories: elite and non-elite. The elite consists of *Thalu, Mahajan*, priest, politicians, and service holder, the commoners are non-elites. The elite here is loosely and broadly defined for those families who possess socio-economic influence or share state power in various capacities.

The elite, in terms of family background, consists of 55 in the total 100 local political leaders. The people with elite family backgrounds dominate the RPP and the NC with their representatives (71 percent and 61 percent) in composition of total 17 and 33 local leaders of these two parties respectively. The CPN-UML is credited with producing its local leaders from the people of non-elitist background. 52 percent of its 44 local leaders is consisted of commoners. One should acknowledge the impact of democracy and democratic process for the emergence of commoners in the leadership position. The aggregate data of 100 local leaders shows that the gap between the elite and non-elite in holding the position of local leadership is narrow by 10 percent, but it is still in favour of the former.

The data on elite or non-elite family background of local leadership of Nepal is very much close to another data regarding their relations with the power structure of the state. The family connection with high power holders has long been considered as an asset for the advancement of political career. Political parties (up from the Parliamentary Constituency Committee), elected bodies (VDC/Municipality, DDC, Parliament/Cabinet) and higher echelon of bureaucracy (including Banks, public corporations, educational institutions) are considered as the main institutions capable of influencing the power politics of the country. Each of 100 sampled local leaders was asked a question—Do your relatives hold post in parties or in elected bodies or in bureaucracy? To those who have relatives working in more areas were requested to identify only one according to their preference. Nearly half of the total 100 respondents gave affirmative answer. It means that they have family connection by blood with the people who enjoy power and position in state authority structures. Around 60 percent of the NC and the RPP local leaders said that their relatives hold posts either in the party or in elected bodies or bureaucracy. But, only 39 percent of 44 local leaders of the CPN-UML has this kind of connection. So the majority of local leaders of this party have neither strong family backgrounds nor power connections. On the contrary, the NC and the RPP local leaders are from elitist family backgrounds and connections with the state power holders. These two factors are considered the ingredients of ascriptive criteria of leadership building. It should be remembered that nearly half of the total 100 local leaders have strong family backgrounds and power connections but the other half have not such privileges. The local leaders were directly asked: To what extent their family backgrounds and power connection contributed to their career advancement? So, it can be assumed that power attracts power in politics as money attracts money in economics.

An attempt was made to find out the proportion of roles played by traditional and non-traditional factors in the emergence of local leadership. The respondents, 100 local leaders, were asked to identify factors (maximum three for each respondent) that contributed to their placement into the leadership position. The possible answers that pre-set 10 contents (family background, economic position, caste/ethnicity, sacrifice, continuity, social reform, *Jan Andolan,* elections and others) can be divided into two broad categories: the first three—family background, economic position and caste/ethnicity—fall under the traditional sources of power, and the remaining factors come under the modern sources of power. The data suggest that the combined strength of all the three traditional sources of power is insignificant in comparison to the role of modern sources of power for leadership building. Though 55 percent local leaders have come from the elite family background, the role of family comes into 5th rank among other sources, which contributed to the emergence of local leadership. This could, therefore, be taken as a conservative figure. Furthermore, one could argue that many leaders hesitate to acknowledge the role of ascriptive factors in their career advancement. But it should also be remembered that 45 percent local leaders have come from the non-elite family. Moreover, the ascriptive factors would have their own influence but they could not play decisive role in selection of political leaders under democracy. They have been severely limited by competitive politics and democratic process in forming political leadership. Factors of political continuity and personality scored highest mark among others, which led to producing political leaders at local level. It suggests that most local leaders of Nepal derive their power and legitimacy from their long service in politics as well as from their own personality. The disaggregate data show that continuity and personality were largely considered in recruitment of local leaders of the NC and the CPN-UML. The RPP differed slightly since the personality counts first and then contribution to social reform in selection of its local leaders.

The integrated data of family background of 100 local leaders shows that 45 percent of them belongs to commoner, followed by 15 percent from service, 13 percent from *Mahajan,* 12 percent from politicians, eight percent from *Thalu,* and 7 percent from priest. This pattern is followed by disaggregate data. Out of 33 NC leaders, 13 belongs to the family of commoner, six to politicians, five to Mahajan, three to Thalu, three to priest, and three to service. Similarly 23 CPN-UML local leaders had come from the commoner, followed by nine from service, four each from priest and politician, two each from *Thalu* and *Mahajan.*

Insofar as relatives in power structure are concerned, majority of them, 20 in 48, are in bureaucracy, followed by party and elected body. The disaggregate data of the NC leaders shows that majority of them, 20 in 33, had relatives in power structure, in party, in bureaucracy, and in elected bodies in order. Only some CPN -UML leaders, 17 out of 44, have their relatives in power apparatus: six in party, six in elected bodies, and five in bureaucracy. 10 RPP leaders said they had relatives in power structure, six are in bureaucracy, three in party and 1 in elected body.

Taking personal capacity as a source of power, the

continuity factor scores high in integrated data, followed by personality (48), social reform (32), family background (22), involvement in the 1990 *Jan Andolan* (16), and active in elections (14). Class and caste factors are least considered. This pattern is applicable to the case of the NC since the continuity factor is considered as the main source of power. Other important sources of power of the NC local leaders are personality and involvement in the 1990 *Jan Andolan*. Continuity remains the major source of power of the CPN-UML leaders too. Personality, sacrifice and social reforms are other sources of their power. Unlike the NC and the CPN-UML, the RPP leaders consider personality and social reform as the first and second sources of power.

Prevalence of non-traditional sources of power in producing political leadership could also be explored from other dimensions—selection of leaders through top-down or bottom-up approach. Leadership building is a complex process in which a number of actors—ranging from local activists to central leaders are involved. In other words, a person to be recruited in leadership position needs internal support from his/her own party leaders and workers. However, very few local leaders, especially of the NC, said they have become leaders by the grace and blessing of the party high command and the central leaders. The local leaders including those of the NC give credit to their own party workers for their selection/election to the leadership position. Does it reflect a general tendency of local leaders that they want to project themselves as popular leaders among the people and the party workers rather than show that they are merely the creatures of the party's top leaders? This is not a complete truth. Rather, it is the manifestation of change in the method of leadership selection, though the NC, the CPN-UML and the RPP are largely considered as centralised parties. In the pre-democracy period and after, almost all-political parties of Nepal selected their own party leaders of different levels through appointment, nomination and consensus.

A reverse change could be observed especially in 1996. This year was marked by the convening of the latest National

Conventions of all the three major parties—the NC, the CPN-UML and the RPP, since most representatives of the National Convention of each party were selected through internal elections. A shift in method of selection of party leaders from nomination to election is an outcome of some developments in party politics of Nepal. The new developments in the NC, the CPN-UML, and the RPP saw factionalism and greater intra-party competition along with erosion of central leadership. Such competitiveness gave rise to intra-party democracy with which to enhance the achievement criteria in leadership building. So the role of the party activists became significant. This new trend is generally reflected in responses of local leaders selected for this study, thus giving more weight to the party workers as an important factor for the election of leadership.

The integrated data of internal support received by 100 local leaders of political parties shows that the support from their own party workers is most vital. Then district level leaders play second important role. Support from high ranking leaders is negligible. The NC local leaders stress the support of party workers for their placement in leadership position. Support from district level leaders and the party high command came next. For the CPN-UML leaders support within the party is crucial. The RPP leaders too give preference to the support of party workers, followed by support of district leaders.

Fifty-eight out of 100 local leaders have used new bases of power by their affiliation with non-political organisations. Organisations which are increasingly becoming favourites of party leaders can be divided into the following types: cultural/religious, education/health, development, social service, professional, human rights and general. Though these are non-political and non-governmental organisations, party leaders tend to expand their support base by cultivating different kinds of civil society groups working in their own localities. The NC local leaders are ahead in using non-political bases of power as 76 percent of its total 33 leaders are affiliated with different type of social organisations, followed by their counterparts of the RPP and the CPN-UML by 59 percent and 43 percent respectively.

The aggregate data of party leaders' affiliation with social organizations show that most of them are involved in education and health sectors, followed by general works, developmental activities, professional works, social service, involvement in cultural/religious and human rights activities. Most NC leaders, 25 in 33, have affiliation with non-political organizations i.e. in social service, general works, education/health services etc. But only some, 19 out of 44 CPN-UML leaders, are involved in non-political organizations such as education /health, development and general. Among the 10 RPP leaders involved in non-political organizations, four are in education/health sectors, two in cultural/religion, two are professional, one involved in development, and one in general works.

Social and economic backgrounds i.e. caste/ethnicity, class, age, occupation etc. are only supporting factors for persons aspiring for leadership positions. The political contribution they have made is the most important aspect for their emergence as political leaders. In a country like Nepal, where political parties originated from and evolved around democracy movement, a person's record of political struggle and sacrifice is considered more important point in recruitment of political leaders. Leaders are generally recruited from amongst those who have long been associated with the party organisation. The constitutions of the NC and the CPN-UML also focus on long apprenticeship in the process of leadership making. According to their constitutions, an ordinary member formally requires his outstanding service to the party at least for two years to be recognised as the active member. Election to the National Convention is a pre-requisite for the candidacy of the NC District Committee presidentship. Only National Council members of the NC and the CPN-UML are eligible for respective Central Committee membership. Yet, no parties seem to strictly follow the respective parties' constitutions.

The restoration of multiparty democracy created an extra-ordinary situation for political parties of Nepal. The RPP had to reorganise the old elites—the former panchas—to form the party. The NC and the CPN-UML had only minimal organisational networks in around 50 districts before 1990, let alone their presence at village level. In the 1992 local elections, each competing party needed 11 candidates in each Village Development Committee and about 50 thousands to contest all seats of around four thousands Village Development Committees, 38 municipalities and 75 District Development Committees. Therefore, they needed local party leaders in large numbers than they had in their own stock. So, the transformation of the NC and the CPN-UML from movement and underground organisations into competitive parties after the restoration of democracy, and their electoral interest led them to adopt a liberal policy in recruitment of local leaders. The NC welcomed into its fold any one who wishes to join it unconditionally and accepted its ideals and values irrespective of their backgrounds. The CPN-UML, in contrast, seem to be looking for different types of people for leadership roles at the local level. Its bias against the former panchas gradually watered down. However, it encouraged the people with old communist background to come and hold leadership position in the party at the local level. It has successfully emerged as the mainstream communist party through the cultivation of a number of leftist leaders defecting from other communist parties both individually and collectively. Many of them are absorbed in the party's various local level posts.

So, the NC, the CPN-UML and the RPP invariably adopt a liberal policy towards recruitment. Their rank and file particularly in lower levels are constituted by a mixed group of people having different political backgrounds. They can be divided into four categories: *early riser*—their association with party began much before the restoration of democracy in 1990. The second category is *prodigals*—those who first socialised in the party and then joined other political groups and came back to the parent party after the restoration of democracy in 1990. The third category is called *converts*. *Converts* are those whose political career started from different political platforms or parties but changed political affiliation after the fall of

TABLE 9
Political Background of Local Leaders

Variables	*NC(33)*	*UML(44)*	*RPP(17)*	*Others(6)*	*Total(100)*
1. Career Beginning (time)					
Before Panchayat (pre-1960)	3	1	1	—	5
Panchayat time (1960-1990)		32	13	5	77
Post-1990 Jan Andolan	27	11	3	1	18
	3				
2. Career beginning from Congress		—	1	2	32
CPN-UML	29	37	—	2	49
Panchayat	1	—	14	2	19
Other Communist parties	3	7	2	—	9
	—				
3. Prison					
No	18	32	15	6	71
Yes, (How Long)	15	12	2	—	29
Less than 1 Year	10	9	2	—	21
1-5 Years	5	3	—	—	8
4. Exile					
No	29	41	17	6	93
Yes, (How Long)	4	3	—	—	7
Less than 1 year	2	3	—	—	5
1-5 Years	2	—	—	—	2
5. Underground					
No		33	16	5	81
Yes, (How Long)	27	11	1	2	19
Less than one year	6	2	1	—	8
1-5 Years	5	7	—	—	8
6-10 Years	1	1	—	—	2
11- above	—	1	—	—	1
	—				
6. Party Swing					
No	29	36	16	3	
Yes (previous group)	4	8	1	3	
Congress	—	1	1	1	
CPN-UML	1	—	—	2	
Panchayat	3	—	—	—	
Other Communist parties	—	7	—	—	

panchayat system. And, finally are the *new comers* who started their political career only after the restoration of democracy. However, parties generally gave preference to the early risers if such people were available.

It is relevant here to state again that political leaders are generally recruited from those who have long association with the political party and made outstanding contributions for the development of party organisation. An attempt is made here to explore the political association and contributions so as to measure the factors of career beginning.

The political career of most local leaders, 82 out of 100, had begun since before the restoration of democracy in Nepal. Over 90 percent NC local leaders were involved in politics before the 1990's political change followed by 78 percent and 75 percent in the case of the RPP and the CPN-UML respectively. One-fourth local leaders of the CPN-UML, 18 percent of the RPP, and 9 percent of the NC are new comers who entered politics recently after the collapse of the panchayat system. It reveals that the CPN-UML has greater ability to absorb new comers. Nevertheless, the generational differences (in term of age) in choice of the party between the Congress and the Communist no longer exist. Above all, the early risers largely constitute the local leadership of these parties.

Thus, the clamour that *Chaite* Congress and *Kartike* communists outnumbered the genuine leaders/workers of the NC and the CPN-UML respectively appears to be only an exaggeration. Those who joined the CPN-UML after the promulgation of the Constitution of the Kingdom of Nepal in the month of *Kartik* (November) 1990 that coincided with the ML's decision to surface from underground politics called *Kartike* communists.

The phrase *Chaite* Congress and *Kartike* communists are coined in negative sense as they have been generally perceived as opportunists. The political background of 100 sampled local leaders suggests different thing against a propaganda that political opportunists have dominated the NC and CPN-UML. Shailaja Acharya, one of the prominent Congress leaders, gave her remark during the party' 10th National Convention, held in Kathmandu in May 1996, that it was a matter of satisfaction that more than 85 percent representatives of the National Convention were those who had already been branded as Congress persons before the restoration of democracy in 1990. This version is indeed substantiated by the data tabulated under the column of "career beginning" and "party- swing". Out of 33 local leaders of the NC, 29 started their career from this party and only 4 came from other parties. Similarly, 37 out of 44 CPN-UML local leaders have continued their association with the CPN-UML. Fourteen out of 17 local leaders of the RPP have begun their career as panchas during the panchayat regime. The record of party swing after 1990 also shows that there are only few converts—four in the NC, eight in the CPN-UML and one in the RPP. Stability in local leadership thus continues because of long political career within their parent organisations.

Most local leaders have good political background due to their long association with their own parties, though many of them have no strong record of political contribution. Only 29 out of 100 local leaders have record of imprisonment for political cause. Nearly half of the NC and the one-fourth of the CPN-UML leaders suffer imprisonment for their past political activities. Only two RPP leaders experience political imprisonment. The Congress and communists were in opposition and hence the strong commitment to the Party is recorded. NC's open politics also made its workers worst sufferers during the partyless regime. In contrast, the communists who worked underground could escape the arrests. Yet, many were killed and imprisoned. Perhaps this is the reason why one-fourth the CPN-UML local leaders experienced underground life, while only six local leaders of the NC have this kind of experience. Besides, only four from the NC and three from the CPN-UML local leaders stayed in exile in the past. The aggregate data of 100 local leaders shows their past political sufferings and struggle with 29 in prison, 19 in underground and seven in exile. It suggests that most of the present local leaders of the NC, the CPN-UML and the

TABLE 10
Socialisation and Motivations of Local Leaders

Variables	*NC(33)*	*UML(44)*	*RPP(17)*	*Others(6)*	*Total(100)*
1. Political Socialisation					
Family	6	4	2	—	12
Peer groups	12	20	10	6	48
Leadership	22	25	11	1	59
Ideology	7	17	1	2	27
Political Events	14	13	2	1	32
Others	5	6	4	1	16
2. Motivation for					
Prestige enhancement	10	8	8	3	29
Community interest	2	1	5	—	8
Social change	19	24	1	3	47
Development	24	29	14	4	71
Uplift backward	7	23	2	3	35
Party Building	10	6	1	2	19
Others	6	15	6	1	28

RPP are just sympathisers or workers of the parties before the 1990. A number of factors work for their motivation in politics.

It needs to be recalled here that most local leaders have begun their political career much before the restoration of democracy in 1990. At the time of their first exposure to politics, two factors—leadership and peer groups—worked as the main source of political socialisation of the NC, the CPN-UML and the RPP local leaders. Though organised politics was prohibited by the Panchayat regime, the party leaders including Panchas were active individually in producing their own followers. Most respondents of this study were educated at school and campus levels. Many of them were exposed to politics for the first time during their student life since the educational institutions provided a platform for "systemic opposition" to the outlawed parties. So the influence of the peer groups for political socialisation was obvious. Each major political force has its own student front: NC's Nepal

Student Union, Communist's All Nepal National Independent Student Union (ANNISU), and the Panchayat's Rastravadi Vidyarthi Mandal. The educational institutions and the student unions served as the main platforms for recruitment to party cadres during the Panchayat period. The local leaders selected for personal interview confirmed it. Almost all the Congress local leaders said in interview that they started their political career as activist of Nepal Student Union. So was the case with the CPN-UML local leaders who started their career in ANNISU.[13] Particular political event is another important source of political socialisation of the NC local leaders, for the CPN-UML local leaders' attraction of ideology seemed to be significant. Only few local leaders of all major parties consider family as the source of political socialisation. Since there was a risk of life if one were to involve in opposition politics during the Panchayat regime, it was understood that the family generally discouraged them for joining opposition politics. Such a trend remains unchanged despite the change of political regime. It is therefore interesting to note why the politician generally prefer to keep their sons and daughters away from politics.

Socialization of total 100 local leaders of political parties was determined by such factors as peer group (48), political events (32) and ideology (27). Among the different factors, political socialization of the NC 33 local leaders can be put in ranking order according to which leadership scored 22 marks, followed by political event (14), peer group (12), ideology (7), family (6) and others (5). Leadership remains the main factor of political socialization of the CPN-UML local leaders, followed by peer group (20), ideology (17), political events (13) etc. For the RPP, leadership and peer groups appear as the main factors of political socialization. Other factors i.e. family, political events, ideology etc. have least role in this regard.

Personal gain and public goods also work as the motivating force for political career. By involving in politics at different

---

13. Baral, *Oppositional Politics in Nepal,* New Delhi : Abhinav, 1977, pp. 145-63.

levels and in various capacities, an individual tries to fulfil his/her personal interest i.e. monetary gains, power, influence and status etc. Interest in public good is another motivating factor, which relates to the people's adherence to the party's ideology, goal and policy. It is already stated that sampled local leaders are involved in politics since the Panchayat time. It can be argued that the personal interest of power and opportunities work as the main source of motivation for panchas when they first joined politics. But, for the NC and Communist leaders, who began their career in opposition politics, their motivation at the initial period was undoubtedly associated with the party's broad ideology and goal. Irrespective of the NC's ideological goal of democratic socialism, it had one-point programme in the past—end of the partyless Panchayat system. So the commitment to multiparty system was the main factor for the early risers of the NC. The personal experience of being victims of the suppression of the regime had turned them rebels. The restoration of multiparty democracy was just a part of the Communist broad ideology of class struggle. So different factors, end of exploitation rather than change of political regime, motivated the CPN-UML local leaders at the time of the beginning of their political career. The information collected through personal interviews with 21 local leaders of different parties found that the motivational factor differed from one party to another. The NC local leaders are motivated to involve in politics both by a combined factor of the Panchayat's suppression and by commitments to the multiparty system. The CPN-UML local leaders are highly motivated by their rebellious spirit against the social and economic exploitation prevailing at that time. On the contrary, power and opportunities then available motivated the RPP local leaders to become regime functionaries. Three representative cases, one from each major party, would be presented here to substantiate what different factors had motivated them to join parties.

Raghubar Bhatta is NC's local leader of Dadeldhura district. He said that a hate feeling against the Panchayat germinated after he was beaten by a group of army-men for his dissent against the discriminatory behaviour in supplying fuel to the army's bus but not to the private vehicles. His own conviction drove him to campaign for the multiparty system in 1980 referendum believing that it would bring about a change.

Lal Bahadur Subba is a local leader of the CPN-UML and Chairman of Ilam District Development Committee. He said that he had become a rebel against social discrimination and exploitation. His desire for radical transformation of society was the main reason for his joining the former ML that subsequently became a major part of the CPN- UML.

Lila Bahadur Dahal is a RPP local leader of Ilam district. He said that he had served the Panchayat system for many years as a bureaucrat holding important posts. He had received opportunity to work with the Panchayat stalwarts i.e. Kirtinidhi Bista, Tulsi Giri and Surya Bahadur Thapa but was impressed by the personality of Thapa. He said that the RPP was his "natural choice".

Most local leaders, irrespective of their party affiliation, identified "development" as their main motivational factor. In the popular imagination, Nepal's development holds a special place. The notion of development is often associated with the process of social change. Thus, the agenda of social change and development became the normative as well as practical motivational factors for the leaders of all shades. Therefore, development and social change seem to motivate most local leaders belonging to the three major parties. Yet, the CPN-UML local leaders present themselves as champions of the backward communities. It was recorded that no parties' local leaders appear to be communal and sectarian.

The integrated data of political motivation of 100 local leaders of the three parties shows that the objective of development was much ahead than others in explaining the reasons behind the involvement in politics. The mission for social change came next as the important motivational factor, followed respectively by commitment to the upliftment of the backward community, prestige enhancement, party building, and promotion of community interest.

Development is identified as the main motivational factor by the NC local leaders, followed by social change (19), party building (10), prestige enhancement (10), uplift the backward groups (7) and community interest (2). For the CPN-UML's local leaders, development remained the main motivational factor. Social change and uplift the backward groups were considered as other significant motivations. Prestige enhancement and party building were considered least for their motivation in adopting politics as their profession. The RPP local leaders also gave preference to development as their key motivational factor. Other motivating factors were prestige enhancement and community interest.

V

LEADERS' PERCEPTION AND PEOPLE'S UNDERSTANDING

Leadership means many things to many people. Leaders are different from the common mass in many respects both in quality and character. So a leader can set norms and values for society. Leaders influence, control and manage their organisations. Leadership in political parties, therefore, is the human face of the party, which largely represents the party's values, ideology, policy and programmes. In this sense, leadership can be considered as an important element of institutions. Leaders are also seen as statesmen on the basis of their responsibility and ability of decision making and crisis management. It is an instrument for social change and economic development.

Central Leaders' Perceptions

The qualitative data collected through interviews with 21 central level leaders, seven from each of the three major parties—the NC, the CPN-UML, and the RPP—suggest that they view the leadership from multidimensional perspectives. In response to a straight question: "What do you mean by leadership and what are the qualities of a good leader," many reply in vague language focusing on personal character, behaviour and leaders' task in national development. They were however categorical in identifying some points related to political leadership. Their perception

TABLE 11
Qualities of Good Leadership as Viewed by Central Level Leaders

Variables	NC	UML	RPP	Total
1. Good Human Being	6	5	5	16
2. Visionary	4	2	4	10
3. Norm and Value Setter	1	1	3	5
4. Party Organiser	1	3	3	7
5. Decision Maker	1	2	2	5
6. Crisis Manager	1	1	3	5
7. Instrument of Social Change and Development	1	1	1	3
8. Service to the People and Nation	2	3	2	7
9. Dedicated to Ideology, Policy and Program	2	3	3	8
10. Others	2	1	1	4

of leaders is given in the Table 11. It is prepared through content analysis of qualitative data.

The aggregate data show that a leader is primarily conceived as a good human being. To become a visionary is the second important quality of a political leader. Thus, leadership is associated with party organiser, dedication to ideological and policy goal, and service to the people and the nation. Leaders as agents of social change and economic development, as the norm and value setter, decision-maker and crisis managers get less consideration. The NC and the RPP central level leaders shared a common perspective with both giving preferences to the quality of good human being and vision. The CPN-UML apex leaders also laid equal emphasis on being good human being as the main quality of leaders but their second preference went to other aspects i.e., party organiser, promoter of party's ideology and policy, and service to the people and nation.

Local Leaders' Perceptions

It should be recalled that parties' central leaders identified the leadership mainly with the quality of good human being rather than with other roles of the leader. Thus, we can

TABLE 12
Local Leaders' Perception of Political Leadership

Variables	NC	UML	RPP	Others	Total
1. Self-Perception					
Personal esteem	10	15	5	2	32
Enlightenment	7	8	1	—	16
Oratory	5	4	1	1	11
Mobilisation capacity	17	20	6	2	45
Sociable	18	27	9	3	57
Selflessness	19	20	11	6	56
Tackling the situation	10	16	8	—	35
Tolerance	5	11	3	3	22
Others	3	1	1	—	5
2. Quality of Respected Local					
Leaders : Good human being	38	60	21	12	131
Commitment to responsibility	8	9	1	1	19
Intellectuality	7	12	8	—	27
Party organiser	20	21	8	1	50
Sacrifice	4	7	1	—	12
Commitment to ideology	4	8	2	2	16
Dedication to development	9	3	4	2	18
Experience	1	1	1	—	3
Others	3	3	3	—	9
3. Quality of Respected National					
Leader : Good human being	19	44	19	6	88
Commitment to responsibility	7	5	1	—	13
Intellectuality	10	24	5	1	40
Party organiser	28	23	9	2	62
Sacrifice	10	5	2	3	20
Commitment to ideology	11	12	4	5	32
Dedication to development	9	6	1	1	17
Experience	2	1	4	—	7
Others	—	6	2	—	8

conclude that the "Trait Approach" is prevailed in their understanding of political leadership. The local leaders and general people also think in this way.

A question was asked to the 100 local level leaders on the basis of the trait approach to an understanding of the leadership phenomena. The question was: How do you (as a leader) generally differentiate between common people and leaders in terms of qualities? Possible answers were pre-set in 9 points (personal esteem, enlightenment, oratory quality, mobilisation capacity, sociable, selflessness, tackling situation, tolerance and others) and each respondent was requested to limit his answers to the three maximum points. The table under the title of self-perception shows that the local leaders of Nepal claimed that sociable and selflessness are the two main qualities they possess as leaders. Others, such as mobilisation capacity, situation tackling capacity and personal esteem come in third ranking, and fourth and fifth qualities in the preferential order. Oratory quality, enlightenment and tolerance scored lowest mark in identification of qualities of local leaders. The disaggregate data suggest that the NC local leaders claimed their strength of selflessness, sociability and mobilisation capacity were in almost equal number and weight. The CPN-UML local leaders considered their sociability as the main asset and selflessness and mobilisation capacity as the second important strengths. Three major qualities of local leaders as seen by the RPP local leaders in preferential order are—selflessness, sociability and situation tackling capacity.

Leadership is not exclusively confined to personal qualities. In addition of being good human being, a true leader must be a party organiser, intellectual, experienced, having record of struggle for cause, committed to development and other responsibility, to mention only a few. An attempt is made to explore multidimensional aspects of leadership. Each of 100 respondents was asked to identify one local and one national leader to whom he/she respected much, and then also to identify three major qualities of such a respected leader. The index of most respected local leaders shows that the main strength of a person they (respondents) regarded highly is his/her quality of good human being. The other reason why the respondents respected a particular person is his/her ability to work as party organiser. The other virtues of leadership i.e. experience, sacrifice, commitment to ideology, dedication to development, and commitment to responsibility figured in less preferential order in counting the qualities of the respondents' respected local leader. The party-wise breakdown of the data also suggest that the NC, the CPN-UML and the RPP respondents share in common that the persons who have quality of becoming good human being and then party organiser were conceived as their (parties' respondents) ideal leaders at local levels.

People's Understanding

In your opinion, what kind of person could be considered as a leader? This straight question was put to 50 citizens of sampled districts randomly. The expected answers were pre-set in eight possible answers—(clean personality, sacrifice, commitment to ideology and goal, contribution to specific political event, ability to manage political crisis, high post holder in party, elected person and others), taking into consideration the multidimensional aspects of leadership. They were further asked to identify their most respected leader, one from local level and other from central level, with follow up questions about three major qualities of their respected leader. Citizen's responses to these questions, presented in the table, manifest peoples' understanding of political leadership.

The data in the table of people's understanding show that leadership is mainly associated with the commitment to ideology and goal. The citizens also treat a person having record of struggle and sacrifice for a cause as a leader. Some emphasised on clean personality to be eligible for leadership. Just holding post either in party or in elected bodies is least considered in defining political leadership. So, a different perspective appears distinctly between the leader's perceptions and people's understanding about leadership. The central and local leaders, selected for this study, mainly equate leadership with the qualities of good human being, visionary, sociable and selflessness. But for people, leaders are those who are committed to ideology and goal and have history of struggle and sacrifices along with clean personality

Yet the distinction between leaders and commoners does not exist much in making points about the qualities of their

TABLE 13
People's Understanding of Political Leadership

Variables	*Respondents (50)*
1. People's Understanding	
Clean personality	22
Sacrifice and struggle	36
Commitment to ideology and goal	40
Contribution in specific political event	4
Ability to manage political crisis	5
High post holder in party	1
Elected person	2
Others	21
2. Quality of Respected Local Leader	
Good human being	76
Commitment to responsibility	10
Intellectuality	14
Party organiser	7
Sacrifice	3
Committed to ideology	7
Dedicated to development	17
Experience	1
Others	3
3. Quality of Respected National Leader	
Good human being	55
Commitment to responsibility	5
Intellectuality	14
Party organiser	22
Sacrifice	10
Commitment to ideology	18
Dedication to development	14
Experience	—
Others	3

respected local and national leaders. Similarly, to the views of political respondents (local leaders), the citizens consider good human being is the main quality of their own respected local and central leaders. Both types of respondents share a common perspective in identifying another important quality as the party organiser. The citizens, however, differed with the political respondents in identifying second important quality of the respect local leader. Unlike the political respondents' second preference to the factor of 'party organiser', citizens see dedication to development as the second important quality of their respected national leaders.

Leadership is an important agent of both political society and civil society. She / He is, therefore, a link between the politics and the people. Political leaders are the main channels of governance. It is the political leadership that mediates between society-party and the state. They articulate the interests of community and group they represent. It is, thus important to know how they articulate the interest they represent.

Interest Articulation

Separate questions were asked to 50 citizens, 100 local leaders and 21 central leaders selected for this survey, about the contents of people's needs, interests and expectations. People's initiation to interact with political leaders was very strong that out of 50 sampled citizens, 46 said that they met political leaders very frequently. They were asked a follow up question: What issue do you raise when you meet political leaders? The people's experience in this regard is cross-checked by asking a question about the contents of people's expectations (expressed during leader-citizens meeting), to each of the 100 sampled local leaders. The possible answers were pre-set into nine contents (favour for job, favour in administrative work, dispute settlement, party affairs, development, social reform and change, community interest, general problems and others) that can be divided into two broad categories: personal interest and public interest. Both types of respondents (citizens and local leaders) were requested to limit their responses to not more than three out of nineidentified topics of people's expectations. The Table 14 shows a comparative data of the citizens and local leaders' version about the nature and contents of societal demand.

The data presented under vertical line of people's view suggests that the issues concerning public interest overwhelm the articulation of citizens' demands with the political leaders.

TABLE 14
People's Demands and Expectations

	Leaders' view					People's view
Variables	*NC*	*UML*	*RPP*	*Other*	*Total*	
1. People's Expectation						
Personal Interest:						
Dispute settlement	21	32	11	5	69	*
Favour for job	20	15	7	1	43	18
Favour in administrative works	21	26	5	4	56	6
Public Interest:						
Party affairs	6	9	4	—	19	10
Development	17	25	11	6	59	30
Social reform and change	—	—	—	—	—	15
Community interest	—	—	—	—	—	5
General issues/ problems	2	8	1	1	12	13
Others	—	3	4	—	3	4

The integrated data of personal and public interests show that the contents of personal interest figure low in people-leaders communications, though people's quest for leader's favour for job come as a second preference. In the list of people's expectations that relate to public interest, the question of development comes first, followed by a demand for social reform/change, issues related to party affairs, community interest and others in preferential order.

The people's version contradicts political leaders' experiences. The rank and file of all major political parties share a common feeling that they have been least pressured to work for general interest of society. Pressure of the people seeking leaders' favour to fulfil their individual and personal interest is high. The table shows that the volume of people's demands that relates to public interest is much lower to personal interest. Development appears as one of the major items in leader-people communication but other issues that benefit larger members of society seldom figure. According to local leaders view, people often seek leaders' favours for their own personal interest i.e., dispute settlement, job and administrative work. The party-wise breakdown of integrated data reconfirm a general tendency that the people seek political favour in return of their vote. People's personal interests such as political backing in dispute settlement, favour for job and administrative work—dominate the volume of people's expectations in the NC. But the pressure for job is negligible for the leaders of the RPP and the CPN-UML since they are not in the government right now. Yet, the local leaders of these opposition parties express that most visitors (people) articulate their own personal interests first than other issues. People's expectations as felt by the CPN-UML leaders are as follows in preferential order: political backing for dispute settlement, administrative work, development, favour for job etc. The RPP local leaders claim that the people who visit their residents and party offices mainly seek political backing for dispute settlement and for development of constituencies.

The central leaders of the NC, the CPN-UML and the RPP have also felt that leader-people relations are dominated by personal interest of individual members of society. It indicates how politics, power, state, government and other institutions are increasingly becoming irrelevant to collective interest of the people and society. Instead, the state machinery and political institutions are manipulated to fulfil personal interests of vested interest groups. This situation is prevailing partly because of the continuation of authoritarian political culture despite a change of political system from partyless Panchayat to multiparty democracy. The people under authoritarian political culture tend to fulfil their personal interests through Chakari to the power holders. So, the resident and office of the influential leaders i.e. MPs, ministers and party leaders etc., are usually crowded with party activists and others, seeking favour for job, promotion, political appointment, contract, deals and other opportunities. The party- sponsored clientalism has further consolidated this system. Change of the government often follows with the change in executive posts at all levels. It affects the working and performance of all organisations and institutions. Ruling party activists and leaders' favourites receive opportunities to be in higher post and position. This also manifests how the leaders distribute patronage. The patronage distribution function is largely guided by personal interest of leaders to consolidate their influence in party politics and in their electoral constituencies. Guided by personal interest to be re-elected next time, politicians, ministers and MPs in particular strive hard in providing services to the voters of their own electoral constituencies. Pattern of patronage distribution has fostered a system—that is like market-exchange system ("vote for favour" and "favour for vote")—in shaping leaders-people relations.

Political parties have now realised that the issues of public concern and national importance are declining in leader-people dialogue. Chitra Lekha Yadav (NC), Deputy Speaker of the House of Representatives and Jog Mehar Shrestha, an influential leader of the RPP, have a common point to say that more than 90 percent visitors, who come to see her/him, seek political backing to fulfil different types of their own personal and individual interests, especially the demand for job is high. Experiences of central leaders of different political parties are

TABLE 15
People's Demands and Expectations

	Central Leaders' view			
Variables	*NC*	*UML*	*RPP*	*Total*
People's Expectation:				
Personal Interest:				
Dispute settlement	1	2	1	4
Favour for job	10	2	6	18
Favour in administrative work	3	1	2	6
Public Interest:				
Party affairs	1	9	3	13
Development	6	2	2	10
Social reform and change	—	2	—	2
Community interest	—	—	—	—
General issues/problems	1	2	1	4
Others	2	1	1	4

presented in table 15. Data is based on the content analysis of the interview taken with central leaders.

The aggregate data reveal that favour for job topped the list of people's expectations followed by other issues—party affairs, development, political favour in administrative work etc. in preferential order. Disaggregate data show some distinction among parties as determined by their own positions in power politics of the country. Since the NC is now a ruling party, its leaders face more pressures for job vis-à-vis people's demands. As the ruling party, the NC has controlled over the state resources, people's expectation for development from the leaders of this party would naturally be high. Being in opposition, the CPN-UML has no patronage distribution capacities now. So, issues related to party affairs dominate the interaction between its leaders and people. In other words, the public contact of the CPN-UML leaders is highly concentrated in their own party clients. The leaders of RPP have also felt that very few come to see them since the party's position has changed from being a partner of ruling coalition in the past into the opposition after the 1999 general elections. Nevertheless, favour for job remains the main demand of those persons who come to see and meet the leaders.The contents of leaders-people communication are largely determined by formal position of party leaders. Experiences of three leaders, each one from the NC, the CPN-UML and the RPP, are presented here as representative cases.

> **Arjun Joshi,** MP of the ruling NC party, said: "People of my constituency want to see me as trouble shooter of all kinds of their individual problems. I am over-pressured by my voters' demands for job and other opportunities. The party activists sometimes ask for political intervention in the cases of sub-judice nature."

> **Dev Raj Ghimire,** MP of CPN-UML said: " As a member of the National Assembly I have realised that I am not directly responsible to the people. I have very limited role in allocation of developmental resources and in other issues of public concern. Besides, since my party

TABLE 16
Responsibilities, Performance, Constraints and Recommendations

Variables	*NC*	*UML*	*RPP*	*Other*	*Total*
1. Responsibilities:					
Party Building	14	19	9	—	42
Institutionalisation (elected body)	12	17	4	3	36
Development	26	34	13	6	79
Social Reformation/change	9	22	7	4	42
Uplift of own community	4	4	4	1	13
Uplift of backward community	4	19	3	1	27
Build democratic culture	13	7	1	—	21
Others	4	1	1	—	5
2. Performances:					
Social service	4	—	3	—	7
Party building	26	21	14	—	61
Uplift of backward community	3	2	3	—	8
Development	40	65	20	9	134
Public awareness	11	8	4	1	24
Favour/recommendation	—	2	—	1	3
Social mobilisation	8	14	3	4	29
Dispute settlement	—	2	—	1	3
Others	2	9	2	2	15
3. Constraints:					
Personal inability	6	10	5	1	22
Undue pressure	2	4	1	4	11
Lack of political will	2	9	3	—	14
Lack of Resources	26	36	9	4	75
Lack of co-ordination	17	24	6	2	49
Non-co-operation	14	16	2	3	35
Inefficient bureaucracy	10	19	2	3	34
Others	6	9	6	—	21
4. Recommendations:					
Training/capacity building	12	20	5	3	40
Restructuring Administration	7	12	1	3	23
Party institutionalisation	9	12	4	—	25
Increase of will power of leadership	19	20	11	3	53
Mobilisation of optimum resources	22	32	9	4	67
Discouragement of abuse of authority	18	19	10	4	51
Others	1	6	—	—	—

is not in power right now, the common people hardly come to see me. So most of my time is spent in party affairs and with party workers."

Mohammed Mohsin, a central leader of the RPP (now the Chairman of the National Assembly) , said : "I am not elected member nor is my party in the government. So, I am not pressurised by the people neither for their individual interest nor for collective interest of society."

Responsibility and Performance

Responsibilities come with the leadership challenges. How leadership takes the responsibility is reflected in the performance results. In this study an open-ended question was asked to all 100 respondents to identify three major responsibilities of leaders that they consider important. (Table 16)

The data under the index of responsibilities suggest that political leadership is very closely associated with the objective of development. The task of party building and social reform/ change received equal importance as the second most important responsibility of political leaders. Institutionalisation of local elected bodies (VDC/Municipality and DDC), uplift of backward community, building of democratic culture etc. has come as other responsibilities in preferential order. Disaggregte data of leaders' responsibility show that the NC local leaders gave emphasis to development, followed by party building, building of democratic culture and institutionalisation of local elected bodies.

The CPN-UML local leaders also perceived that development is their main responsibility but the second and third priorities were given to social reform/change, party building and uplift of backward community respectively. Unlike their Congress counterparts, the CPN-UML local leaders gave least preference to institutionalisation of local elected bodies and to building of democratic culture. The local leaders of the RPP stand close to their counterparts of the CPN-UML while identifying development, party building and social reform/change as their first, second, and third important responsibilities respectively.

Do the local leaders' perceived responsibilities match their performance? There is a close correlation between the leaders' perceived responsibilities and self-evaluation for their performance. The data show that development receive highest mark in the index of responsibilities and performance of local leaders. Leadership is, therefore, intertwined with development. The task of party building is second important job in terms of responsibility and performance of local leaders. Other contributions made by local leaders, as they claimed, are the following in preferential order: social mobilisation, public awareness etc. They felt that they have been highly pressurised by people's individual interest i.e., favour for dispute settlement, job and administrative work, but local leaders' responses to people's personal demands get less preferential treatment in the index of local leader's performance. Social service and work for uplifting the backward community are least noticed by local leaders while recalling their functions. Nevertheless, the CPN-UML local leaders perceive the uplift of the backward community as their third important responsibility. The disaggregate data of the local leaders' performances are very close to party-wise breakdown of local leaders' perceived responsibilities. Development, party building and public awareness receive first, second and third positions in the NC local leaders' performance list. For the RPP local leaders too, development and party building remain agendas of their contributions. The priorities listed in the CPN-UML local leaders' performance index are development, party building and social mobilisation respectively.

As the contents of performance are concerned, some similar and some different pictures appear between the local and central leaders. The list of performance made by 21 sampled central level leaders, as they told while replying to a question (Identify three major works done in capacity of political leader?), is presented in table 17 through content analysis of qualitative data.

The aggregate data suggest that development and party building scored high preference in the list of central leaders'

TABLE 17
Performance of Central Leaders

Variables	*NC*	*UML*	*RPP*	*Total*
Struggle for democracy	6	—	—	6
Social service	—	—	1	1
Party building	2	13	3	18
Uplift of disadvantaged sections of society	4	2	2	8
Development	5	4	11	20
Institutionalisation of democracy	1	—	1	2
Promotion of nationalism	—	—	1	1
Others	3	1	2	6

performance. It is similar to the case of local leaders. But, party-wise breakdown of data shows a different picture. For the NC central leaders, struggle for democracy has come as the main point to score in listing their major works. Other works performed by the NC central leaders in preferential order are: development, uplift of the backward community etc. The CPN-UML central leaders have few things to say about major works they have done, but they all stressed more on their own contribution to party building. Development counts a lot in performance list of the RPP central leaders. The disaggregate data show a clear difference among central leaders of major political parties vis-à-vis their performance: struggle for democracy scored high in performance list of the NC central leaders; party building in the CPN-UML; and development in the RPP. Such a distinction speaks different histories of three parties. The present leaders of the RPP were experienced rulers under the past partyless Panchayat System (1960-90). So they have many things to recall about development works undertaken in the past under their own initiation. What Balaram Gharti Magar (one of the Panchayat stalwarts who headed various ministries for long time) said, could be a representative case:

> Before I was first elected to the National Panchayat in 1962 from Rolpa district, there was only one post office (Hulak) in my district. Now you can see post offices in each VDCs of this district. About 200 schools are

> established under my leadership. Drinking water is available to all villages. Telephone facility is there. Several health posts and one hospital have already been established. The motorable roads connect the headquarter and thousands of bridges are constructed. All these development activities have been undertaken under my leadership.

Organisation building has always been the priority of communist parties before and after the restoration of democracy. In the last 10 years of democracy, the CPN-UML was in power for a short time (nine months as the single party minority government and as partner in coalition governments formed under the leadership of the RPP and the NC). So its leaders have only few things to register in the list of performances they have made. The CPN-UML rank and file believe that they could reach power mainly through organisation building. So party building is always a priority for its members. The experience of Til Kumar Meyoungbo, an MP of CPN-UML from Taplejung district, is an example. He said:

> "What remarkable works I have done till now is exclusively related to expansion and strengthening of my own party. Particularly when our party split in 1998 with the emergence of the CPN (ML) as a separate party, I was able to bring most party workers of Taplejung district to the fold of the CPN-UML. The split has, therefore, least impact in Taplejung district; the CPN-UML remains strong in my district as it was before the split. So this is my great political achievement and contribution".

The NC had launched several movements for democracy, some times peacefully and some times violently. The party and its leaders are thus over-conscious of their history of struggle and sufferings when they talk about their performance. This is well reflected in reply of Sushil Koirala, General Secretary of the party, to the question—What are the three major works you have done in the capacity of a leader? He said:

> "Democracy is my mission. So the restoration of multiparty system is my first great achievement. I have constantly followed the principles and ideals set by the late B.P. Koirala and this is my second achievement. Third, I am working hard for the consolidation and institutionalisation of democracy in Nepal".

In fact, central leaders of all the three major parties are largely overburdened by the histories of their own respective parties rather than by the need of present time while talking about their performances. They did not associate themselves with particular value system, specific policy and task, except three women (Chitra Lekha Yadav of the NC, Shanta Manabi of the CPN-UML and Roshan Karki of the RPP) who correlated their role of political leadership with their missions of women empowerment. Sunil Kumar Bhandari of the NC is another exception who specifically rationalised his work in family planning and in initiating the abortion right. Uplifting other disadvantaged sections of society i.e. untouchable, bonded labour etc. is counted in performance of only a few leaders. If development activities undertaken in the past by the RPP central leaders is excluded from the table, development becomes one of the neglected areas in the index of leaders' performances. No-development would have strong negative impact on the legitimacy and credibility of political leaders. All the 42 political leaders—21 from local level and other 21 from central level—selected for interview of this study have a common voice in saying that the credibility of political leaders is declining considerably.

Since none of them disagreed with this general conclusion, the distinction according to party affiliation and hierarchy (local and central) is not made here. They identify several factors that lead to the decline of the credibility of Nepali political leaders. Their points of view, as they told during the interview, are developed in tabular form through content analysis of qualitative data.

Leaders of different political parties confess that a number of inter-related factors have led to the decline of the credibility of political leadership in Nepal. One of the main reasons is the gap between leaders' promise and their performance. The

TABLE 18
Factors Leading to Decline of Political Leaders' Credibility

Variables	*Leaders' views*
Gap between promise and performance	30
Lack of performance	12
Lack of clear vision	4
selfish and corrupt	36
Promoting valueless/normless politics	24
In-party factionalism	6
Promotion of nepotism/favouritism	10
Others	4

conclusion of three general elections and two local elections within 10 years of democracy has given rise to taste for populist politics. The parties and candidates make high promises for development to attract the votes but they have not been supported by their performances. It would have negative repercussion on parties and leaders. Dev Raj Ghimere of the CPN-UML explained how the credibility of his party, if not popularity, has been lost: "In the initial phase of democracy we raised people's expectations to attract them. We tried to give an impression to the party workers and sympathisers that radical changes would occur soon. But national and international environments are quite different from our target. A favourable situation may come up in the future but people will not have patience to wait for long". Part of the reason behind the gap between leaders' promise and their performance can be found in limited resources of the country. But the problem also lies in motivation of political leaders.

In Nepal, leaders have become synonymous with selfishness and corruption. Leaders in this study share this general feeling. According to them, the main reason for decline of leaders' credibility is that there is a general tendency, among leaders, to grab resources and opportunities by all possible means, moral or immoral, ethical or unethical and legal or illegal, for their own personal interests. So the moral standard of Nepali politics has reached the lowest point. Dhundi Raj Shastri of the NC observed: "Credibility of political leaders are declining rapidly because the rank and file of all political parties have used politics as an instrument to fulfil their own personal interest rather than use it (politics) for the benefit of people, society and nation".

Since a tendency of promoting self-interest is rampant among the leaders, they are consciously or unconsciously contributing to the erosion of value and ideology in politics. While identifying increase of valueless and normless politics as third major reason for the decline of leaders' credibility, the respondents of this study seem to be preoccupied with unhealthy trends of dirty politics that visibly appeared during the time of hung-parliament and coalition politics (November 1994 to May 1999). Bribe, horse-trading, blackmail, abduction of some unreliable incumbent ministers and law makers, conspiracy, manipulation of constitutional loopholes appeared as the order of politics during the coalition time. No substantial changes have seen to be made after the emergence of majority government of the NC after the May 1999 parliamentary elections. The erosion of value in politics is not arrested with seriousness. Other factors leading to the decline of leaders' credibility are: lack of performance, promotion of nepotism and favouritism, lack of clear vision and perspectives, and increasing internal factionalism within political parties.

The individual components of leaders i.e. character, behaviour, interest etc. are the key factors leading to decline the credibility of political leaders generally. This is reconfirmed by 100 sampled local level leaders while replying to a separate question about the strength and weakness of Nepali leaders.

Data in the index of weaknesses show that the portraits of Nepali political leaders are selfish and corrupt. Their other characteristics, in preferential order, are power centric, deviation from norm and value, negligence of people and development, promotion of nepotism and favouritism, confinement to party interest, and negligence of national interest. The disaggregate data also expose their weakness. In the eyes of NC local leaders, political leaders are mainly selfish and corrupt followed by other characteristics: power centric, uncommitted to value-based politics etc. Similarly, the

TABLE 19
Strength and Weakness of Political Leadership

Variables	*NC*	*UML*	*RPP*	*Others*	*Total*
1. Strength					
Ability to build consensus	9	4	5	1	19
Commitment to democracy	17	22	4	2	45
Consciousness for Development	15	24	3	5	47
Leadership quality	15	19	7	3	44
Accommodative/ adaptability	7	6	2	1	16
Nationalist	4	8	2	1	15
Record of sacrifice, experience	4	4	2	—	10
Others	—	1	—	—	1
2. Weakness:					
Selfish and corrupt	31	59	19	4	113
Power centric	18	13	10	2	43
Confine to narrow party interest	5	9	1	2	17
Neglect of national interest	6	6	1	1	14
Promoting nepotism, favouritism	6	8	4	1	19
Deviation from norm/value/ ideology	10	15	5	1	31
Negligence of people and development	8	8	6	2	24
Abuse of authority	—	1	—	1	2
Others	1	3	2	2	8

CPN-UML local leaders perceive leaders as mainly selfish and corrupt, uncommitted to value-based politics, and power centric. According to local leaders, political leaders are selfish and corrupt, power centric, lack of commitment to the people and development.

The sampled local leaders hardly referred individual qualities when they talk about the strength of Nepali political leaders. Their main strength is realisation of their weakness and commitment to the need of development to regain legitimacy. They are committed to democracy, which indicates integration of most political parties under the mainstream parliamentary procedure irrespective of their past ideological backgrounds. They have also some qualities i.e. history of political struggle, elected from people, post-holders in parties etc. to be qualified as a leader. The ideological convergence has positive contribution to making pragmatic leaders of different political parties. Their ability to build inter-party consensus is increasing. Disaggregate data suggest that the NC local leaders perceive that commitment to democracy, development and leadership quality are the main strengths of political leaders. This opinion is more or less shared by the CPN-UML local leaders. They count on consciousness of development, commitment to democracy and leadership quality as the first, second and the third strengths of political leadership. Leadership quality, ability to build consciousness and commitment to democracy as the first three important strengths were also recorded. Much strength of political leaders seems to be a by-product of political integration of parties and processes as underway for the last ten years. But leader's weakness lies more in their personal character and narrow individual interest.

Personal character, behaviour and change in motivation of leaders have obstructed them to discharge their responsibilities. Other constraints are no less significant for neutralising their performance. In response to a question to identify three major constraints facing political leaders, the respondents of 100 sampled local leaders identified a number of constraint variables.

The data presented in the index of constraint show that

TABLE 20
Major Constraints Facing Party Leaders

Variables:	*No.*
Personal inability	22
Under pressure from party	11
Lack of political will	14
Lack of resources	75
Lack of coordination within party	49
Non-cooperation from other parties	35
Inefficient bureaucracy	34
Others	21

lack of much needed resources is the main problem faced by the leaders. Other constraints in priority order are: lack of co-ordination within party, non-co-operation from other parties, inefficient bureaucracy, personal inability, lack of political will and undue pressure from party. Such a general view is more or less applied to each party. The NC, the CPN-UML and the RPP local leaders share a common perspective in identifying the lack of resources and lack of co-ordination within their parties as the first and second major constraints. Non-cooperation from other parties is conceived as the third major constraint by the NC local leaders, but inefficient bureaucracy figures in the CPN-UML local leaders' lists.

These constraints can be mitigated if proper measures are taken by the parties. Each of 100 sampled local leaders is requested to provide maximum three recommendations for the improvement of quality and ability of political leaders of Nepal.

The data in the index of recommendations show that emphasis is given to mobilisation of much needed resources. It should be referred that lack of resources is considered is the main constraint. So there is close correlation between the identification of main problems and recommendations. Lack of co-ordination within party and non-co-operation from other parties have been taken as the second and third important problems. Institutionalisation of political party and party system could be a proper answer to these problems, but this

TABLE 21
Recommendations for Mitigating Constraints

Variables:	*No.*
Training/capacity building	40
Restructure of administration	23
Party institutionalisation	25
Increase of will power of leaders	53
Mobilization of optimum resources	67
Discouragement of abuse of authority	51
Others	7

is considered as least important in the index of recommendations. Similarly, lack of political will is taken as one of the least important constraints but the local leaders stress the increase of will power of leadership as the second important measure. Discouragement to abuse of authority is another significant aspect recommended by the local leaders. Disaggregate data show that there are commonalties between the NC and the CPN-UML local leaders in their recommendations, putting mobilisation of resources, increase will power of leadership and discouragement to abuse of authority as first, second and third important measures respectively. The RPP Local leaders also gave equal emphasis to these three measures, though with slight differences in preferential order.

Of the 21 central leader selected for this study, each was requested to give his/her recommendations (maximum 3) for the improvement of leadership quality in Nepal. Their points of views were organised through content analysis of qualitative data and are presented in the table 22.

Several recommendations made by party central leaders are categorised into above mentioned (in table) six contents. They consider the need of regaining personal honesty and character as the first major remedy to resolve the problems of political leaders of Nepal. The next important recommendations they have made for the institutionalisation of political parties and political process. Another aspect noticed by central level leaders is the need for accountability to the people. A

TABLE 22
Recommendations of Central Leaders

Variables	*NC*	*UML*	*RPP*	*Total*
Regain of personal honesty and character	6	9	8	23
To be responsible/accountable to people	2	2	3	7
Pressure of civil society	2	—	2	4
Reward and punishment system	3	2	1	6
Institutionalisation of parties and political process	4	5	2	11
Others	1	1	2	4

system of reward and punishment should be introduced to safeguard the accountability. Disaggregate data show that the central leaders of all political parties realise in common that the first important thing is personal honesty and character of leaders. The NC and the CPN-UML leaders gave second importance to the need of institutionalisation of parties and political process, but for the RPP, to be responsible and accountable to the people is more important. Most central leaders agree on the role and pressure from society as the important elements for improving the quality of politics and political parties.

VI

CONCLUSION

Leadership is a crucial variable for the development of democracy and the country. Without strong commitment to development and institutionalisation of political process, no country can prosper. Related to it are also the issues of effective governance. In the developing country like Nepal, it seems that every aspect of country's development boils down to the leadership role. With this underlined assumption, this study has tried to explore the emergence and dynamics of both central and local leaders under the present democratic dispensation.

The major parties like the NC and the CPN-UML have the trends of continuity and change, though in the former case, old leaders are still considered to be the backbones of the organisation. The continuity of local leaders who had been working in various parties earlier during the Panchayat period provide the parties with strong base as most of them have continued working within their respective organisations rather than switching loyalties to others. Even changing party positions, they have chosen another party or parties, which are identified with similar ideologies. The split of the CPN-UML showed such a trend when deserting party members preferred to join the CPN (ML). In this context, the situation in the RPP is slightly different because of its past background. Only a limited number of party members did change their political loyalty by joining the NC.

Another factor observed by this study is the low

representation of women in general because of the scant attention being paid by political parties' to women empowerment. In absence of vigorous women movement to be mounted by some committed women leaders, male dominated social and economic structures of the Nepali society can hardly come up to the expectation of the women. It has been noticed that women represented in the parliament and in different hierarchies of their respective parties tend to be identified more with parties than with women movement. Conceivably, all major parties have the same ratio of women representation in elected posts at both local and central levels. Caste, family links and other forms of patronage routes equally figure in accommodating women in various organs of government and parties.

Ethnic imbalance is another feature of leadership situation in Nepal. All the data generated and the documentary evidences show that the same caste groups have dominant positions in various layers of parties and elected bodies. However, it is interesting to know that no ethnic and other forms of communal, sectarian and regional platforms outside the political parties have been able to win elections to various posts at both central and local levels. During the three parliamentary elections, such non-partisan platforms could hardly make any dent in electoral politics. Political parties, it would appear, have been able to accommodate various ethnic and regional groups making candidates at various levels. Yet, so far as the sociological balance is concerned, Nepali political process has to go a long way in the direction of bridging the gap between the high castes and other groups.

The study also found out that the 55 percent local leaders have come from the elite family background. However, the role of family was considered less important by the respondents. This could be attributed to many leaders who hesitate to acknowledge the role of ascriptive factors in their making. The data show some changes in leadership emergence as 45 percent of local leaders come from non-elite family background. In 1999 general elections to 205 members of the House of Representatives, more than two-thirds representatives are new comers. It is indeed a good sign of emergence of new leaders in Nepali politics. The circulation of elites in accordance with the established procedures and timeframe are also the conducive aspects of leadership building process in an evolving democracy.

The growth of leadership is facilitated by the competitive political processes introduced at all levels of political system and parties. Whatever flaws and aberrations are detected can be rectified only through the dynamics of competitive politics. Nepal's progress is therefore not at all disappointing despite the continued trends of caste, *chakari*, personality and family dominated political culture. The country's historical legacy, authoritarian and feudalistic orientation of elites seem to have seeped through the arteries and veins of party leaders thus contrasting their long political backgrounds and sufferings for the cause they were believed to have upheld. Now they are in the vortex of competition that put them in defensive if their behaviours and actions go wrong. Since the process of more competition and introspection has just begun, it is premature to infer any conclusion about the failure of democratic process itself. Nevertheless, the competition that prepares leaders would not be adequate for sustaining democracy if leaders in government and outside fail to provide good governance. In Nepal, political leaders stress much on formal structures than on the essence of participatory democracy.

Finally, perceptions of Nepali voters and their leaders are not necessarily congruent as these perceptions are inter-mingling. The central leaders of some parties under review think that the people are always kind by showing their compliance to them, while the people want them to be exemplary or role models. Intellectuals on their side want to see their leaders as innovative, responsive, dynamic, transparent, dedicated and clean. But when such ideal attributes are absent, they become utterly frustrated.

The central level leaders of the three parties under this study have shown that many of them would lose their importance once they were defeated in elections showing that their legitimacy is very much determined by their posts or status they hold after winning elections. If some senior leaders lose parliamentary elections, their chances of becoming ministers, Prime minister and leaders are remote. Neither they show strong popular base out of office, nor are they involved in mobilisation of party workers. The defeated NC leaders seem to be particularly affected by electoral setbacks. One of the principal reasons of such a trend is that the second, third or fourth generation of leaders depend too much on senior leaders for their career building rather than engage themselves in organisational matters. Political parties are the vehicles of democracy and leadership is an integral part of it. If parties fail to be institutionalised by their built-in mechanisms, norms and leaders' commitment, their ad hoc nature and functions continue to plague them. Sometimes, leaders create institutions, but normally, institutions help create, socialise and train leaders. The present study has tried to investigate into such interactive and contributory roles of these two aspects of leadership and institution building. The existing picture however seems to be fuzzy in determining which element is more striking in leadership building in Nepal. A few more years of democratic exercises would be able to show how far parties and other institutions would go to producing leaders at all levels.

SELECT BIBLIOGRAPHY

Abullaish, *Effectiveness of Local Leadership for Change and Transformation of Rural Society*, Kathmandu: CEDA/TU, 1982.

Agrawal, Govind R., *Decentralization for Rural Development in Nepal* (Monograph), Kathmandu: CEDA,Tribhuvan University, 1986.

Apter, David, *introduction To Political Analysis*, Cambridge: Massachusetts, Winthrop, 1970.

Bacharach, Peter, *The Theroy of Democratic Elitism: A Critique*, London: University of London Press Limited, 1969.

Baral, Lok Raj, *Pattern of Representation in the National Panchayat of Nepal*, Kathmandu: INAS/TU, 1975.

.............., " Democracy, Leadership Role and Nation Building in Nepal" in Dhruba Kumar, ed., *State Leadership And Politics in Nepal*, Kathmandu: CNAS/TU,1995.

.............., "The First Panchayat General Election in Nepal", *The Nepalese Journal of Political Science*, Vol.VI, No.2, December 1981.

.............., *Nepal's Politics of Referendum: A Study of Groups, Personalities and Trends*. Delhi: Vikas, 1983.

.............., *Oppositional Politics In Nepal*, New Delhi: Abhinav, 1977.

.............., *Village Politics and Development: A Study of Three Village Panchayats* (Unpublished Memo), Kathmandu: CNAS/TU, 1978;

.............., "Nepal: Local Politics and Some Trends of Social Change", *Indian Journal of Nepalese Studies*, Vol.1, July-December 1987.

Baral, L.S. "The First Panchayat Elections in Nepal, 1962-63: The Emergence of A New Political Generation", *International*

Studies, Vol.12, January-December 1973.

Barman, Dalem Ch., *Emerging Leadership Pattern in Rural Bangladesh* (Unpublished Ph.D.Thesis) Jaipur: University of Rajsthan, 1983.

Bhargava, B.S., *Grassroot Leadership: A Study of Leadership in Panchayat Raj Institutions*, New Delhi: Ashish Publishing House, 1979.

Bhattachan, Krishna B., "Ethnopolitics and Ethno-development: An Emerging Paradism in Nepal", in Dhruba Kumar, ed., *State, Leadership and Politics in Nepal*, Kathmandu: CNAS/TU, 1995.

Bhattarai, Lok Krishna, "Kamyunist Andolanma Sahi Pakshyako Uthan" (Rise of Real Section in Communist Movement), *Kantipur Daily*, December 1, 1999.

Bista, Dor Bahadur "*Fatalism and Development: Nepal's Struggle for Modernization*", Calcutta: Orient Longman, 1991.

Blondel, Jean, *Political Leadership: Towards a General Analysis* London: Sage , 1987.

Borgstrom, Bengt-Erik, *The Patron and the Panca: Village Values and Panchayat Democracy in Nepal*, New Delhi: Vikash Publishing House, 1980.

Borre, Ole, et. al., *Nepalase Political Behaviour:* New Delhi, Sterling, 1994.

Bottomore, T.B., *Elites and Society*, London: Penguin 1964.

Bowman, Lewis and Boynton, G.R., "Activities and Role Definitions of Grassroots Party Officials", *Journal Of Politics*, February 1966.

Burns, James MacGregor, *Leadership*, New York: Harper & Row, 1978.

Caplan, Lionel, *Administration and Politics in a Nepalese Town: The Study of a District Capital and its environs*, London: Oxford University Press, 1975.

Chalise, Suresh C., " The Social Background of Legislative Elite in Nepal, 1986", *Indian Journal of Nepalese Politics*, Vol.1, July-December 1987.

.............., *Sociology of The Legislative Elite In A Developing Society*, Kathmandu: Nepal Foundation for Advanced Studies, 1995.

Chauhan, R.S., *The Political Development in Nepal 1950-70: Conflict Between Tradition and Modernity*, New Delhi: Associated Publishing House, 1971.

Dahal, Dilli Ram, "Nepal's Governing Elite: Their composition and Role in Constituting the State", paper presented in a national seminar on *Domestic Conflicts and Crisis of Governability in Nepal,* organised by the CNAS on November 17-18, 1998.

.... , "Ethnic Cauldron, Demography and Minority Politics: The Case of Nepal", Dhruba Kumar, ed., *State, Leadership and Politics in Nepal,* Kathmandu:CNAS/TU, 1995.

Dahl, Robert. A., "Hierarchy, Democracy, And Bargaining In Politics And Economics" in Heinz Eulau , et.al. eds, *Political Behavior,* New York: The Macmillan, 1956 (Indian. edn. 1972).

DREFDEN, *Report on the Study and Research on the Local Elections in Nepal 1992,* Kathmandu: DREFDEN, 1992, p.7.

Duverger, Maurice, *Political Parties,* New York: John Wiley and Sons, 1954.

Edinger, Lewis J. *Political Leadership in Industralized Societies: Studies in Comparative Analysis,* New York: John Wiley and Sons, 1967.

Eldersveld, Samuel J. *Political Parties: A Behavioural Analysis,* Chicago: Rand NcNally, 1964.

Gaige, Federick H, *Regionalism and National Unity in Nepal,* New Delhi: Vikas Publishing House,1975.

Gardner, Howard, *Leading Mind,* New York: Basic Books, 1995.

Golam Hoosain, A.K.M. *Bangladesh Nationalist Party: A Political Analysis* (Unpublished Ph.D.Thesis), Rajasthan: University of Rajasthan, 1984.

Gupta, Anirudha, *Politics in Nepal: A Study of Post-Rana Political Developments and Party Politics,* Bombay: Allied Publishers, 1964.

Gurung, Harka, "Representing An Ethnic Mosaic", *Himal,* May/ June 1992.

.... , "Sociology of Elections in Nepal, 1959-1981" *Asian Survey,* Vol. XXIV, No. 3, March 1982.

.... , Social Demography and Expressions, Kathmandu: New Era, 1998.

Harvard Business School, 1989.

Huntington, Samuel P., *Political Order in Changing Societies,* New Haven, Conn.: University Press, 1968.

IIDS, *The Second Parliamentary Election: A Study of Emerging Democratic Process in Nepal,* Kathmandu: IIDS, 1993.

Jahan, *Rounaq, Bangladesh Politics: Problems and Issues,* Dhaka: University Press Ltd., 1980.

Joshi, Bhuwan Lal and Rose,Leo E., *Democratic Innovations in Nepal: A Case Study of Political Acculturation,* Berkeley: University of California Press, 1966.

Khatri, Sridhar K., *Political Parties and Parliamentary Process In Nepal: A Study of the Transitional Phase,* Kathmandu: Political Science Association of Nepal, 1992.

Kochanek, Stanley A., *The Congress Party of India: The Dynamics of One-Party Democracy,* Princeton: Princeton University Press, 1968.

Kohli, Atul *Democracy and Discontent: India's Growing Crisis of Governability,* Cambridge: Cambridge University Press, 1991.

Lane, Robert E., *Political Ideology,* New York: The Free Press, 1962.

Lawson, Kay, *Comparative Study of Political Parties,* New York: St. Martin Press, 1976.

Michael, Robert, *Political Parties: A Sociological Study of the Oligarchical Tendencies of Modern Democracy,* New York: The Free Press, 1968.

Panebianco, Angelo, *Political Parties : Organization and Power,* London: Cambridge University Press, 1988.

Pant, Dipak Raj, " Higher Education and Liberal Values in Nepal", *European Bulletin of Himaliyan Research,* No.9, 1995.

POLSAN, *Nepalases Voters: A Survey Report,* Kathmandu: POLSAN, 1991.

Poudyal, Ananta Raj, " Nepal: Ethnicity in Democracy" in Lok Raj Baral, ed., *South Asia: Democracy and the Road Ahead,* Kathmandu: POLSAN, 1992.

............., *Nation Building in Nepal: A Case Study of the Post Revolution Period 1950-1981* (Unpublished Ph.D.Thesis), Kathmandu: Tribhuvan University, 1986;

Putnam, Robert D., *The Comparative Study of Political Elites,* New Jersey: Prentice-Hall, Inc., 1976.

Rana, Pashupati Shumsher and Mohammad Mohsin, *A Study Report on the Pattern of Emerging Leadership in Panchayets,* Kathmandu: CEDA/TU, 1967.

Rawal, Bhim, *Nepalma Samyabadi Andolan: yashko Udbhab, Vikas ra Bartaman Abastha,* (Communist Movements in Nepal: Its Origin, Development and Present Situation), Nepal: Samana Prakashan, 1984.

Regmi, Mahesh C., *Kings and Political Leaders of Gurkhali Empire 1768-1814,* Hyderabad: Orient Longman, 1995.

Right, William E. ed, *A Comparative Study of Party Organization,* Ohio: Carles E. Merrill Publishing Company, 1971.

Rose, Leo E., "Communism Under High Atmospheric Conditions:

The Party in Nepal " in Robert A. Scalapino, ed., *The Communist Revolution in Asia,* New Jersey: Prentice-Hall, 1965.

Seligman, Lester G, "The Study of Political Leadership" in Heinz Eulau, et al. *Eds., Political Behaviour,* NY: The Macmillan, 1956.

Shaha, Rishikesh, "The Nepalese Ministerial Elite Since 1960: Change and Continuity of the Political Elite" *The Nepalese Elite,* Banaras: Center for the Study of Nepal, 1982.

.............., *Essays in the Practice of government in Nepal,* Delhi: Manohar, 1982.

.............., *Politics in Nepal: 1980-1991,*New Delhi: Manohar, 1993.

Sharma, P.R., "Nepali Culture and Society: Reflections on Some Historical Currents" in Kamal P. Malla, ed., *Nepal: Perspectives on Continuity and Change,* Kathmandu: CNAS/TU, 1989.

.............., "Bahuns In the Nepali State", *Himal* , 7:2: 1994.

.............., " Ethnicity and National Integration in Nepal: A Statement of the Problem", *Journal of Nepalese Studies,* Vol. 1, July-December 1987.

.............., "How to Tend This Garden" *Himal,* May/June 1992.

SHTREE SHAKTI, *National Gender Analysis on Elected and Nominated Women Ward Representatives,* Kathmandu: UNDP, 1998.

Siriskar, V.M., *The Ruling Elite in a Developing Society,* New Delhi: Orient Longmans Ltd., 1970.

Stodgill, Ralph M., *Leadership,* Oxford: London, 1997.

The Constitution of the Communist Party of Nepal (Unified Marxist-Leninist).

Toole, James O., *Leading Change,* London: Jossey-Bass, 1995.

Tripathi, Satyendra, " Political Elite and Their Strategies in Nepal", *The Nepalese Elite,* Banaras: Center for the Study of Nepal, 1982.

Weiner, Myron, *Party Building in a New Nation: The Indian National Congress,* Chicago: University of Chicago Press, 1967.

Yukl, G, *Leadership in Organisation* (3rd edn.), NJ: Englewood Cliffs, 1994.

INDEX